Psalm 119:
Lessons for Life

By
Elaine Jordan

ISBN-10: 1-58427-541-3

ISBN-13: 978-1-58427-541-1

All photos and graphics are from istockphoto.com or the public domain.

Truth Publications, Inc.
CEI Bookstore
220 S. Marion St., Athens, AL 35611
855-492-6657
sales@truthpublications.com
www.truthbooks.com

Table of Contents

Author's Notes and Acknowledgments

Special thanks to, Kim McKay who gave these lessons a test drive and helped me with her insights and corrections of the lessons. Since the 2020 year of Covid quarantine prevented their use in home Bible classes, as a way to "test them out," her help was invaluable. Thank you, Kim!

Thank you to my Bible class ladies, too. Even though we could not be together, your encouragement is unflagging and fuels my aspiration to write lessons.

I have used the New King James Version of the Bible for my lesson quotes. I hope you enjoy this translation.

Overview

Lesson 1: Overview

The Book of Psalms

The book of Psalms is a collection of 150 poems and songs written by several Old Testament authors and divided into five books. Moses probably wrote the earliest psalm in the 15th century BC and Ezra, the latest one in the 5th century BC. Also, researchers believe Ezra compiled the book of Psalms into the five books that we see today. The psalms express the author's deepest passions, including despair, confessions, great joy, and praise of God. No matter if the psalm tells of joy or sorrow, it leads the reader to hope and praise God. The book itself is mentioned twice in the New Testament, Luke 20:42 and Acts 1:30.

Now David himself said in the book of Psalms: "The Lord said to my Lord, "Sit at My right hand, till I make Your enemies Your footstool" (Luke 20:42–43).

For it is written in the book of Psalms: "Let his dwelling place be desolate, And let no one live in it"; and, "Let another take his office" (Acts 1:20).

The word "psalm" is derived from the Greek word *psallō,* meaning to touch or pluck as a hair or beard and also, to touch or pluck a string. The word is applied to instruments of music employed in praise and to general acts of praise. As a noun, the word refers to a song accompanying stringed instruments, and specifically a song of praise to God. As a verb, it means praise.

Authors of Psalms

The authors of Psalms lived throughout Jewish history. In many psalms, the author of the psalm is named in an introductory notation. Some believe that Ezra added these notations later to aid in the interpretation of the psalms.

David may have authored the most with 66 to 75 psalms (number varies depending on the scholar), mainly in the first, second, and fifth books that comprise collections of psalms. He may also be the author of psalms when no author is named as he was an excellent poet and musician.

Other noted authors of psalms are Asaph, the conductor of David's choir of the temple (12 psalms), sons of Korah (10 psalms), Solomon (2 psalms), Moses (1 psalm), Ethan (1 psalm), and Heman (1 psalm). The Septuagint translation notes some psalms were written by Jeremiah,

Ezekiel, Haggai, and Zechariah. These notations may be conjecture as the notes were not in the Hebrew text.

Fifty psalms have no named author. Sometimes the authorship of these psalms is attributed to a particular person elsewhere in the Bible. For instance, 2 Samuel 22 records Psalm 18 as David's, with only slight variations. David has a medley recorded in 1 Chronicles 16:8–36, which has parts of Psalm 105:1–15 and 106:47–48. Psalms 2, 95, and 110 are attributed to David in the New Testament.

Timeline of Psalms

The book of Psalms was written throughout Jewish history, from Moses's time to the return of captivity, with authors from each age. Moses wrote Psalm 90. The last psalms were written in the 5th century BC, as they refer to the Babylonian captivity.

David wrote most of the psalms and introduced singing in the temple *(1 Chron. 25)* during his reign (1010–970 BC). King David ordered proper worship for the Lord: *"Moreover David and the captains of the army separated for the service some sons of Asaph, of Heman, and of Jeduthun, who should prophesy with harps, stringed instruments, and cymbals" (1 Chron. 25:1).* Note that the word prophesy means any divinely authorized utterance or deed. Authorized music is a form of prophesying. The rest of chapter 25 delineates specific duties related to temple music and responsible families.

Hezekiah referred to David's commandment as part of temple worship, which reinforces David's influence in the book of Psalms:

And he stationed the Levites in the house of the Lord with cymbals, with stringed instruments, and with harps, according to the commandment of David, of Gad the king's seer, and of Nathan the prophet; for thus was the commandment of the Lord by His prophets. The Levites stood with the instruments of David, and the priests with the trumpets. Then Hezekiah commanded them to offer the burnt offering on the altar. And when the burnt offering began, the song of the Lord also began, with the trumpets and with the instruments of David, king of Israel. So all the assembly worshiped, the singers sang, and the trumpeters sounded; all this continued until the burnt offering was finished. And when they had finished offering, the king and all who were present with him bowed

and worshiped. Moreover, King Hezekiah and the leaders commanded the Levites to sing praise to the Lord with the words of David and of Asaph the seer. So they sang praises with gladness, and they bowed their heads and worshiped (2 Chron. 29:25–30).

Ezra was the high priest and scribe during the rebuilding of the temple after the Babylonian captivity. He is credited with collecting and arranging the 150 psalms into the books and order as we have them today.

Purpose of Psalms

God-fearing people wrote each psalm to reflect sentiments and situations in which they found themselves. The psalm might be a prayer or a confession. Joy, praise, despair, and darkness are all found in Psalms, but God's presence is constant in each one. God's love and grace are the hope of each writer.

There is a prophetic nature to many psalms. Specifically, Psalm 16, 22, 24, 40, 68, 69, and 118 are called messianic psalms. However, the New Testament quotes other psalms with messianic purpose. Nearly half of all messianic references in the New Testament have origins in the book of Psalms.

Acts 13:33

God has fulfilled this for us their children, in that He has raised up Jesus. As it is also written in the second Psalm: "You are My Son, Today I have begotten You."

It is taken from Psalm 2:7, which says, *"I will declare the decree: The Lord has said to Me, 'You are My Son, Today I have begotten You.'"*

Hebrews 2:6–9

But one testified in a certain place, saying: "What is man that You are mindful of him, Or the son of man that You take care of him? You have made him a little lower than the angels; You have crowned him with glory and honor, and set him over the works of Your hands. You have put all things in subjection under his feet." For in that He put all in subjection under him, He left nothing that is not put under him. But now we do not yet see all things put under him. But we see Jesus, who was made a little lower than the angels, for the suffering of death crowned with glory and honor, that He, by the grace of God, might taste death for everyone."

It is derived from Psalm 8:6, which reads, "You have made him to have dominion over the works of Your hands; You have put all things under his feet."

John 13:18

I do not speak concerning all of you. I know whom I have chosen; but that the Scripture may be fulfilled, "He who eats bread with Me has lifted up his heel against Me."

It is derived from Psalm 41:9, which reads, "Even my own familiar friend in whom I trusted, Who ate my bread, Has lifted up his heel against me."

Hebrews 1:8

But to the Son He says: "Your throne, O God, is forever and ever; A scepter of righteousness is the scepter of Your kingdom."

It is derived from Psalm 45:6, which reads, "Your throne, O God, is forever and ever; A scepter of righteousness is the scepter of Your kingdom."

Matthew 22:44 and Hebrews 1:13

The Lord said to my Lord, "Sit at My right hand, Till I make Your enemies Your footstool."

But to which of the angels has He ever said: "Sit at My right hand, Till I make Your enemies Your footstool"?

They are derived from Psalm 110:1, which reads, "The Lord said to my Lord, 'Sit at My right hand, Till I make Your enemies Your footstool.'"

Organization of Psalms

The book of Psalms is divided into five collections. Most scholars agree that these collections, as we know them, were collected and published after the return from exile. However, the psalms were composed and arranged (and maybe edited). over a long time. The Holy Spirit inspired and oversaw all.

The first psalm in each collection introduces the book's theme, and the last psalm concludes with praises.

Book One: Psalms 1–41

Mostly written by David.

The theme is the separation of the just from the unjust.

Psalm 1 is entitled, "The Way of the Righteous and the End of the Un-godly," which happens to be Book One's theme.

Psalm 41 praises God, who is merciful to sinful man and knows the just and unjust.

Jehovah is named approximately 275 times as God-fearing man calls upon and praises God.

Book Two: Psalms 42–72

Mostly written by David.

The theme is the sufferings of the just ones who cry to God.

Psalm 42 is entitled, "Yearning for God in the Midst of Distresses," and states this collection's theme.

In Psalm 72, Solomon sings of the glory of the Messiah's reign. These psalms let us see that God is with us in our sufferings and that His power is forever.

Book Three: Psalms 73–89

Mostly written by Asaph and sons of Korah.

The theme is the return of Israel as a people and God's mercy for His people.

Psalm 73 is entitled, "The Tragedy of the Wicked, and the Blessedness of Trust in God."

Psalm 89 celebrates God's covenant with David and mourns that David's descendants were not faithful. The author of Psalm 89, Ethan the Ezrahite, implores God's mercy for all of David's descendants.

Book Four: Psalms 90–106

Mostly anonymous authors, with a few by David and others. The theme is security living close to God. Psalm 90 is entitled, "The Eternity of God and Man's Frailty." This collection was written for public worship, mostly by unnamed authors, and does not indicate when or where they were written. Psalm 106 ends with the following words, affirming the promises from God and praises to God are true.

Blessed be the Lord God of Israel From everlasting to everlasting! And let all the people say, "Amen!" Praise the Lord!

Book Five: Psalms 107–150

Mostly anonymous authors, with a few by David and others. The theme is a summary of God's dealings with His people and praise for His mercy. Psalm 107 is entitled, "Thanksgiving to the Lord for His Great Works of Deliverance." Psalm 150 praises God. The repeated commands to praise God in this psalm are a fitting ending to the book of Psalms.

Categories of Psalms

Psalms are often categorized by the author's point of view or by the requests made to God in the psalm.

Royal psalms: Emphasize God as King and often point forward to the coming of Jesus.

Psalms of Zion: Focus on Jerusalem.

Penitential psalms: Confess sin and ask for forgiveness, resulting in praises for God's forgiveness.

Wisdom psalms: Contrast righteousness and wickedness.

Torah psalms: Focus on the beauty, truth, and sufficiency of the Law of God.

Creation psalms: Praise God as Creator.

History psalms: Recount Jewish history and ask for a renewed commitment to God.

Imprecatory psalms: Call for curses upon the wicked.

Passover psalms: Celebrate the great acts of God.

Hallel psalms: Praise God for His character and saving works. *Hallel* is the principal Hebrew word for praise.

Characteristics of Psalms

When studying the book of Psalms, it is essential to remember that the psalms were sung, particularly as part of public worship in Old Testament times. Psalms convey the deep feelings of righteous people to and about God. As such, psalms include deeply emotional language, dramatic exaggeration, and figurative speech to express the utterances from their souls. These feelings may be joyous, reflective, despondent, or triumphant.

Ordinary Life

The writing of psalms was part of ordinary Hebrew life. Hebrew poetry is always religious in nature and not designed for frivolity or festive amusements. At times, the Israelites (or Hebrews) spontaneously responded to the Lord with a psalm of praise. Consider Moses and the Israelites (Exod. 15), Deborah (Judg. 5), Hannah (1 Sam. 2), David (1 Chron. 29), and Mary (Luke 1).

Even when a psalm began as a private song to God, it became part of public worship. Psalms all lead the reader or singer to God, whether it started as a personal song or for public worship. Today, Christians use psalms in both public worship and private devotionals.

Another characteristic to be remembered when reading or studying the book of Psalms is psalms are Hebrew poetry. Hebrew poetry has no rhyme, rhythm, or meter, as modern poems often do. Still, there are features in Hebrew poetry that help the reader understand and appreciate the psalm's meaning.

Alliteration

Alliteration is when the beginning of words is similar and not the ending of the words. Psalms 9, 10, 25, 34, 37, 111, 112, 119, and 145 have each verse beginning with a successive letter of the Hebrew alphabet. Alliteration is also found in Lamentations 1, 2, and 3.

Comparisons

Authors often associated their situation or feelings with an image to help the reader picture their thoughts or circumstances. For example:

He shall be like a tree planted by the rivers of water, that brings forth its fruit in its season, whose leaf also shall not wither; and whatever he does shall prosper (Ps. 1:3).

Many bulls have surrounded Me; Strong bulls of Bashan have encircled Me. They gape at Me with their mouths, Like a raging and roaring lion. I am poured out like water, And all My bones are out of joint; My heart is like wax; It has melted within Me. My strength is dried up like a potsherd, And My tongue clings to My jaws; You have brought Me to the dust of death. For dogs have surrounded Me; The congregation of the wicked has enclosed Me. They pierced My hands and My feet (Ps. 22:12–16).

Parallelism

Parallelism is the repetition of a statement for emphasis.

- **Synonymous parallelism**—Different words repeat the same thought.

Hear this, all peoples; Give ear, all inhabitants of the world (Ps. 49:1).

- **Antithetic parallelism**—Contrast in the final clause stresses the thought of the first sentence.

For the Lord knows the way of the righteous, but the way of the ungodly shall perish (Ps. 1:6).

- **Synthetic parallelism**—Final clause completes and expands the thought of the first sentence.

Our fathers trusted in You; they trusted, and You delivered them (Ps. 22:4).

Psalm 119

Psalm 119 is in the praise psalms of book five. This psalm celebrates God's law in 176 verses and is the longest psalm in the book of Psalms. Scholars debate whether this psalm was written by David or during the time of Ezra and Nehemiah.

Psalm 119 is an acrostic psalm and has twenty-two paragraphs—one paragraph for each of the 22 Hebrew consonants with eight verses in each section. Each line of the eight verses begins with that Hebrew consonant.

Psalm 119 has at least ten synonyms for God's law—law, word, saying, commandment, state, ordinance, precept, testimony, way, and path. Some scholars include the word *truth* in this list. The reader should not assume that God's law is only the Torah. God's law consists of the Scriptures as a whole. Jesus and the apostles often quoted or alluded to Old Testament verses. For example:

- Psalm 35:19, Psalm 69:4, and Psalm 109:3–5 are quoted in John 15:25.

But this happened that the word might be fulfilled which is written in their law, "They hated Me without a cause" (John 15:25).

- Isaiah 28:11–12 is referenced in 1 Corinthians 14:21.

In the law it is written: "With men of other tongues and other lips I will speak to this people; and yet, for all that, they will not hear Me, " says the Lord (1 Cor. 14:21).

The general subject of Psalm 119 is God as a way of life. God sanctifies the soul, God is our support in trials, God brings happiness, and God deserves obedience. Psalm 119 teaches that faithful people should consider God's law in their youth, during their trials, as their duty, in their thoughts, at night, in public, in private, in good times, and in bad times.

The remaining lessons in this book do not attempt to study all thoughts expressed in Psalm 119. They select certain verses to develop specific ideas into a lesson for detailed study. However, Psalm 119 has a myriad of lessons for development!

Sources

Barnes, Albert. *Albert Barnes' Notes on the Whole Bible: Psalms.* StudyLight.org, London: Blackie & Son, 1870–1872. https://www.studylight.org/commentaries/eng/bnb/psalms.html.

———. *Albert Barnes' Notes on the Whole Bible: Psalms.* StudyLight.org, London: Blackie & Son, 1870–1872. https://www.studylight.org/commentaries/eng/bnb/psalms–119.html.

Coffman, James Burton. *Coffman Commentaries on the Bible: Psalms.* StudyLight.org, Abilene Christian University Press 1974. https://www.studylight.org/commentaries/eng/bcc/psalms.html.

"Introduction to the Book of Psalms." *NKJV Study Bible: Second Edition.* Nashville, TN: Thomas Nelson Publishers, 2012.

Remmers, Arend. *Coffman Commentaries on the Bible: Book Overview of the Psalms by Arend Remmers.* StudyLight.org, Abilene Christian University Press 1974. https://www.studylight.org/commentaries/eng/bcc/psalms.html.

Discussion Questions

1. What is the value of studying the book of Psalm?

2. If Ezra added the author notations, does that lessen the value of the psalms? Why or why not?

3. How can poems that were written thousands of years ago be relevant to Christians today?

4. How do imprecatory psalms harmonize with the gospel's teaching of love?

5. What psalm has "spoken" to you, and why was it helpful?

6. The book of Psalms is organized into five collections. The Torah is the first five books of the Old Testament. Is there a correlation? If yes, what is it?

7. What feelings or situations are pictures in Psalm 1:3 and Psalm 22:12–16?

8. Why is it hard today to study the book of Psalms as poetry?

9. Why is parallelism significant when studying the Bible?

10. What are some characteristics that make Psalm 119 different from other psalms?

Playing by the Rules

Blessed are those who keep His testimonies, who seek Him with the whole heart (Ps. 119:2).

Lesson 2: Playing by the Rules

What is a rule? Webster's Dictionary says a rule is a prescribed guide for conduct or action. Rules can be so simple that a four-year-old can play "Go Fish" or be the law of a nation or a governing authority's regulations. There are rewards for observing the rules and penalties for disobeying them. The psalmist of Psalm 119 used the word testimonies for God's rules. He tells us blessings are for those who keep God's testimonies and seek God with their whole heart.

Lance Armstrong was a sports icon for his seven consecutive Tour de France victories from 1999 to 2005. Disobeying the rules forever tar-

nished his reputation. Mr. Armstrong was stripped of all of his achievements from August 1998 onward for using performance-enhancing drugs. The World Anti-Doping Code, which oversees competitive cycling, absolutely forbids the utilization of all performance-enhancing drugs in all sports. This scandal ended Mr. Armstrong's competitive cycling career.

Similarly, Ben Johnson did not play by the rules for track and field. Mr. Johnson had won so many races that he was invested as a Member of the Order of Canada in 1987. Mr. Johnson continued to win races and became a lucrative marketing celebrity. During the 1988 Summer Olympics in Seoul, Mr. Johnson won the 100-meter sprint but was stripped of his gold medal three days later for using forbidden performance-enhancing drugs. Mr. Johnson went from hero to zero!

Not all sports heroes are rule-breakers. Michael Phelps is the most successful and most decorated Olympian of all time, with twenty-eight medals. He also won multiple medals during World Championship, Pan Pacific, and US competitions. Mr. Phelps was a vocal anti-performance-enhancing-drug swimmer. He volunteered to be tested more than the

World Anti-Doping Agency guidelines and passed all tests during the 2008 Olympics. Mr. Phelps trained and swam with focus and determination to win his races. His legacy is untarnished and intact because he swam by the rules.

God's Rules

God has rules for His followers, too. Like the World Anti-Doping Code is accessible to athletes to ensure compliance, God's rules are always available to His followers.

At the beginning of time, God spoke directly to the patriarchs to tell them what He wanted them to do. During Moses's time, God's rules were written down and made known to all His people. These detailed laws and regulations guided how the Israelites were to live and worship. All the people could know what God's rules were, not just the priests. God required His people to be set apart and distinguishable from others due to their holy living. Today, we have God's new covenant, a new set of rules containing the gospel message.

There have always been consequences for disobeying God's rules. Adam and Eve walked in the garden with God. God had given them jobs to do and rules by which to live.

Then the Lord God took the man and put him in the Garden of Eden to tend and keep it. And the Lord God commanded the man, saying, "Of every tree of the garden you may freely eat; but of the tree of the knowledge of good and evil you shall not eat, for in the day that you eat of it you shall surely die" (Gen. 2:15–17).

Most everyone knows the rest of this story. Adam and Eve ate from the tree of the knowledge of good and evil. God drove them from the garden and placed cherubim to guard it *(Gen. 3:1–24).* Adam and Eve broke God's rules and had to endure the repercussions of their action.

Noah is the opposite example. He spent 100 years building an ark because God commanded it. Noah and his family lived after the flood because of their obedience *(Heb. 11:7).*

There are always consequences for obedience and disobedience of God's word. Each person gets to choose which they will do.

Faith before Obedience

Faith is required to obey God's rules. After all, why would anyone pay any attention to God's commandments when they have no faith in God or Jesus? Webster's Dictionary defines faith as confidence or trust in something. The Bible defines faith as the substance of things hoped for, the evidence of things not seen *(Heb. 11:1)*. Persons with faith in God and Jesus are sure that God will keep His promises and obey Him for that reason.

Through Him we have received grace and apostleship for obedience to the faith among all nations for His name *(Rom. 1:5)*.

Hebrews 11 also mentions the faith of many heroes of the Old Testament.

By faith Abel offered to God a more excellent sacrifice than Cain, through which he obtained witness that he was righteous, God testifying of his gifts; and through it he being dead still speaks *(v. 4)*.

By faith Enoch was taken away so that he did not see death, "and was not found, because God had taken him"; for before he was taken he had this testimony, that he pleased God *(v. 5)*.

By faith Noah, being divinely warned of things not yet seen, moved with godly fear, prepared an ark for the saving of his household, by which he condemned the world and became heir of the righteousness which is according to faith (v. 7).

By faith Abraham obeyed when he was called to go out to the place which he would receive as an inheritance. And he went out, not knowing where he was going (v. 8).

By faith Sarah herself also received strength to conceive seed, and she bore a child when she was past the age, because she judged Him faithful who had promised (v. 11).

By faith Abraham, when he was tested, offered up Isaac, and he who had received the promises offered up his only begotten son (v. 17).

By faith Isaac blessed Jacob and Esau concerning things to come (v. 20).

By faith Jacob, when he was dying, blessed each of the sons of Joseph, and worshiped, leaning on the top of his staff (v. 21).

By faith Joseph, when he was dying, made mention of the departure of the children of Israel, and gave instructions concerning his bones (v. 22).

By faith Moses, when he became of age, refused to be called the son of Pharaoh's daughter… esteeming the reproach of Christ greater riches than the treasures in Egypt; for he looked to the reward (vv. 24, 26).

These heroes are not the only ones mentioned in Hebrews 11, just some for this lesson.

For each, their faith caused them to be obedient to God's commands. This cause and effect are what we must emulate. Our faith results in our obedience to God's commandments—the cause and effect. The heroes of Hebrews 11 knew this truth.

But without faith it is impossible to please Him, for he who comes to God must believe that He is, and that He is a rewarder of those who diligently seek Him (Heb. 11:6).

Diligently seeking God is learning about and obeying God. Because of their faith, the heroes of Hebrews 11 were obedient to God's commandments and would receive all God's promises.

Our Faith and Obedience Receiving God's Promises

Jesus Was Obedient

The New Testament urges Christians to obey God's rules and commandments throughout its chapters. In Jesus's life, we see that He was obedient to God as well. Many times, He told His audience that He was speaking God's words and with God's authority. For example, Jesus affirmed His obedience to a gathered crowd in Jerusalem after His triumphal entry.

For I have not spoken on My own authority; but the Father who sent Me gave Me a command, what I should say and what I should speak. And I know that His command is everlasting life. Therefore, whatever I speak, just as the Father has told Me, so I speak (John 12:49–50).

In the Garden of Gethsemane, Jesus prayed, "Your will be done" *(Matt. 26:42b).* Jesus obeyed God when He knew His submission involved pain and suffering.

Obey God Rather than Men

Christians are set apart from the world. God does not mean for His people to blend in with all the people of the world. Our obedience to Him distinguishes us from worldly people. Our actions, clothes, charity, demeanor, and ethics all reflect God. Our desire to integrate with popular culture is natural, and Satan is whispering about the advantages of fitting in. However, God demands that we listen to Him and conform to His commands and not the world's mores.

The Sanhedrin arrested Peter and John because Peter and John preached about Jesus's resurrection in the temple. The Sanhedrin commanded them not to speak at all nor teach in the name of Jesus. Peter and John were faithful and obedient apostles of God. Their reply to the powerful Sanhedrin Council was, "Whether it is right in the sight of God to listen to you more than to God, you judge. For we cannot but speak the things which we have seen and heard" *(Acts 4:19b–20).* Peter and John had to preach what God wanted them to say!

All the apostles continued to preach the gospel boldly in the temple. The high priest and the Sadducees had all the apostles arrested and put in the common prison. During the night, an angel released them and told them, "Go, stand in the temple and speak to the people all the words of this life" *(Acts 5:20)*. So early the next morning, the apostles entered the temple and began preaching! Of course, the high priest and Sadducees were incensed at this turn of events and demanded why the apostles were disobeying the command never to preach about Jesus nor mention His name. The apostles' reply must be our reply in similar situations.

> *But Peter and the other apostles answered and said: "We ought to obey God rather than men"* *(Acts 5:29)*.

The apostles were obedient to God even when threatened by the high priest, prison time, and beatings. We Christians must be as faithful in our daily lives. Our choices may not be as dramatic as the apostles' above situations, but are not necessarily different and certainly not less important. Our decisions are part of daily life. We are obedient to God when we do not cheat on tests, pay our taxes, dress modestly, worship on Sunday, and help others. We may not stand in front of a hostile crowd, affirming that we must obey God rather than men. However, we must be prepared to do so.

Our Obedience Shows Our Faith

The world gives us many reasons to follow popular trends. Often the popular trends are the wide gates of Jesus's parable in Matthew 7:13–14. The one reason for obedience to God is to show our faith in God.

Now by this we know that we know Him, if we keep His commandments. He who says, "I know Him, " and does not keep His commandments, is a liar, and the truth is not in him. But whoever keeps His word, truly the love of God is perfected in him. By this we know that we are in Him. He who says he abides in Him ought himself also to walk just as He walked (1 John 2:3–6).

John tells us that our faith in God is evident because we keep God's commandments. What a novel concept! When we love and believe in God, we do what God says. We obey all the commandments, not only the ones we like or the easy ones.

All of us know people who say they believe in God, but they do not know God's word and His commandments. John calls these people "liars." Acknowledging God is not the same as faith in God. Faithful people keep God's commandments.

By this we know that we love the children of God, when we love God and keep His commandments. For this is the love of God, that we keep His commandments. And His commandments are not burdensome. For whatever is born of God overcomes the world. And this is the victory that has overcome the world—our faith (1 John 5:2–4).

The Obedient Receive God's Promises

Faith results in obedience, which leads to receiving God's promises. In New Testament times, the winning athletes received a laurel crown. Our laurel crown for running the race of life with obedient faith is the crown of righteousness.

For I am already being poured out as a drink offering, and the time of my departure is at hand. I have fought the good fight, I have finished the race, I have kept the faith. Finally, there is laid up for me the crown of righteousness, which the Lord, the righteous Judge, will give to me on that day, and not to me only but also to all who have loved His appearing (2 Tim. 4:6–8).

Paul writes these words at the end of his life. He had obeyed, persevered, and served God until the end. He did not lay on his laurels before he had finished the race. Our race lasts until our life is over, and then we receive the crown of righteousness for our reward.

Summary

And also, if anyone competes in athletics, he is not crowned unless he competes according to the rules (2 Tim. 2:5).

Just as athletes must compete according to the rules, Christians must obey God's commandments. The athlete cannot receive the prize without following the rules of the game. Similarly, a Christian cannot receive God's promise without obedience to God's commandments.

Sources

https://en.wikipedia.org/wiki/1988_Summer_Olympics.

https://en.wikipedia.org/wiki/Ben_Johnson_(Canadian_sprinter).

https://en.wikipedia.org/wiki/Lance_Armstrong.

https://en.wikipedia.org/wiki/List_of_multiple_Olympic_medalists.

https://en.wikipedia.org/wiki/Michael_Phelps.

https://en.wikipedia.org/wiki/Order_of_Canada.

https://en.wikipedia.org/wiki/Tour_de_France.

Discussion Questions

1. Why are athletes common examples for Christians?

2. How has God made His rules known to people in the past?

   How do we know God's rules today?

3. Why are the heroes of faith in Hebrews 11 relevant today?

4. How are faith and obedience related to a Christian?

5. Why is it important to know Jesus was obedient to God?

6. How can we know when the world's laws contradict God's laws?

7. How do our daily choices reflect our obedience to God's commandments?

8. Why is acknowledging God not the same as faith in God?

9. What does God promise to those who are faithful and obedient?

10. How do Paul's admonitions in 2 Timothy encourage Christians?

Seeking and Heeding God's Way

How can a young man cleanse his way? By taking heed according to Your word (Ps. 119:9).

Lesson 3: Seeking and Heeding God's Way

The second paragraph of Psalm 119 starts with a question. How can a young man cleanse his way? *(Ps. 119:9a).* The same verse immediately answers this simple question. By taking heed according to Your word *(Ps. 119:9b).*

A young man can cleanse his way and be righteous before God by heeding and obeying God's word! Notice the following verses of this paragraph tell the young man how to heed and obey God's word. The author wanted all readers to know how to please God!

With my whole heart I have sought You; Oh, let me not wander from Your commandments! Your word I have hidden in my heart, That I might not sin against You. Blessed are You, O Lord! Teach me Your statutes. With my lips I have declared All the judgments of Your mouth. I have rejoiced in the way of Your testimonies, As much as in all riches. I will meditate on Your precepts, And contemplate Your ways. I will delight myself in Your statutes; I will not forget Your word (Ps. 119:10-16).

These phrases summarize the above verses: seek God, make God's word a part of you, listen and teach about God, find joy in God's word, and think about God daily. These phrases start with action verbs: seek, make, listen, teach, find, and think. A young man or any person must actively pursue a righteous life to be pleasing to God.

Seek God

In the Sermon on the Mount, Jesus emphasized that God must be the priority in our lives. God must come before food, clothing, and shelter, which are the basics of everyday living on earth.

Therefore, do not worry, saying, "What shall we eat?" or "What shall we drink?" or "What shall we wear?" For after all these things the Gentiles seek. For your heavenly Father knows that you need all these things. But

seek first the kingdom of God and His righteousness, and all these things shall be added to you. Therefore do not worry about tomorrow, for tomorrow will worry about its own things. Sufficient for the day is its own trouble (Matt. 6:31–34).

Yes, we need food, clothing, and shelter, or we perish for lack of those basics. However, that is only our earthly shell that dies. God promises us eternal life with Him when we have lived our earthly lives righteously. We need God more and must strive for higher things than our earthly lives. James 4:14 tells us that life is "vapor that appears for a little time and then vanishes away." Our earthly lives are short! Eternity with God lasts forever!

Eternity with God comes to those who actively seek God and take heed according to His word.

Make God's Word a Part of You

God's word is part of you when He is the priority in your life, and His word is integral to your daily living. If we have not hidden God's word in our hearts *(Ps. 119:11),* how can we be righteous before God?

In the Sermon on the Mount, Jesus teaches, "Blessed are those who hunger and thirst for righteousness, for they shall be filled" *(Matt. 5:6).* Psalm 119:11 teaches us the same thing. People who hunger and thirst for righteousness have devoured God's word to feed their souls. Similarly, hiding God's word in your heart means His commands are part of your innermost being and thoughts. God's commands guide your choices when His word is part of your daily living. This guidance causes us to desire to please God and to be righteous before God.

The law of his God is in his heart; none of his steps shall slide (Ps. 37:31).

None of this can happen if you do not know what God's word contains! The only way to know is to spend time in the word. There is no pill to swallow, giving us instant knowledge. Time and effort are required from each person to understand and digest God's word before we can hide it in our hearts.

We must actively feed on God's word and hide it in our hearts to be righteous before God.

Listen and Teach

The young man of Psalm 119 asked to be taught God's commandments and promised to declare God's law with his mouth. Of course, the young man cannot learn anything if he will not listen. We Christians have a comparable commandment to teach and proclaim the

gospel. Similarly, unbelievers must listen to and learn the gospel message.

And He said to them, "Go into all the world and preach the gospel to every creature. He who believes and is baptized will be saved; but he who does not believe will be condemned (Mark 16:15–16).

The gospel is the good news of Christ's plan of salvation for the entire world. Jesus commands all Christians to teach and preach the gospel. People who listened can learn God's commandments. This pattern is as the young man proclaimed in Psalm 119.

Preaching the gospel and listening to God's word lead to believing. Believing the gospel leads to obeying the gospel. The young man of Psalm 119 understood the essence of Jesus' command to spread the gospel message of salvation. Hearing, listening, believing, obeying, and teaching becomes a cycle within the gospel plan.

We must first hear the gospel to know about salvation. Then we must listen to what we have heard to obey God's commands. Hearing perceives the sounds of the teaching of the gospel. Listening analyzes the sounds consciously for the understanding of the meaning. So we must first hear the gospel message to listen and understand it.

So then faith comes by hearing, and hearing by the word of God (Rom. 10:17).

Hearing is followed by listening and understanding the gospel. Belief and obedience then follow listening and understanding. Jesus wanted people to listen, believe, and obey the gospel.

Jesus came to Galilee, preaching the gospel of the kingdom of God, and saying, "The time is fulfilled, and the kingdom of God is at hand. Repent, and believe in the gospel" (Mark 1:14b–15).

He who believes and is baptized will be saved; but he who does not believe will be condemned (Mark 16:16).

Jesus's gospel plan of salvation is for all to believe and obey. If Christians who believe do not teach those who have not heard, how can the unbelievers understand what they must do?

For this is good and acceptable in the sight of God our Savior, who desires all men to be saved and to come to the knowledge of the truth.

For there is one God and one Mediator between God and men, the Man Christ Jesus (1 Tim. 2:3–5).

After we have heard, listened, and obeyed the gospel, Jesus commands us to teach others. Mark 16:15–16 commands believers to teach the entire world about the gospel. God commands Christians to continue the cycle—teaching, hearing, listening, believing, obeying, teaching, hearing, listening, believing, obeying, etc. The process continues until all people have heard the gospel and have the opportunity to obey.

Christians must actively listen to learn and to teach God's gospel plan of salvation.

Find Joy in God's Word

The young man of Psalm 119 rejoices in God's word more than the riches of the world. He values God more than gold and silver because he understood that he could not serve both God and wealth. Jesus taught the same thing in the Sermon on the Mount.

Do not lay up for yourselves treasures on earth, where moth and rust destroy and where thieves break in and steal; but lay up for yourselves

treasures in heaven, where neither moth nor rust destroys and where thieves do not break in and steal. For where your treasure is, there your heart will be also (Matt. 6:19–21).

All of us are aware of people who have more money than they could ever spend in their lifetime. Their passion and drive is the accumulation of wealth. The funny thing is a tombstone marks a rich person's grave just as a poor person and others will enjoy their wealth after their death. Jesus teaches this thought in a parable.

Then He spoke a parable to them, saying: "The ground of a certain rich man yielded plentifully. And he thought within himself, saying, "What shall I do, since I have no room to store my crops?" So he said, "I will do this: I will pull down my barns and build greater, and there I will store all my crops and my goods. And I will say to my soul, "Soul, you have many goods laid up for many years; take your ease; eat, drink, and be merry." But God said to him, "Fool! This night your soul will be required of you; then whose will those things be which you have provided?" So is he who lays up treasure for himself, and is not rich toward God (Luke 12:16–21).

Instead of joy in earthly riches and our present comfort, Jesus teaches Christians to find joy in the gospel. Our priority is God and not our worldly assets. A time will come when the demands of the world will conflict with the commandments of God. Those whose lord is earthly wealth may find those demands oppose God's commandments.

No one can serve two masters; for either he will hate the one and love the other, or else he will be loyal to the one and despise the other. You cannot serve God and mammon (Matt. 6:24).

Christians actively find joy in God's word and lay up their treasures in heaven.

Think about God

The young man of Psalm 119 promised God to meditate on His precepts and to contemplate His ways. What does this promise mean?

- **Meditate** means to think deeply and carefully about something.
- **Contemplate** means to think profoundly and at length.

- **Precept**s are God's laws and commandments.
- **Ways** are the characteristics, conduct, or thinking of and by God.

The young man had promised to think deeply, carefully, and at length about God's laws and commandments and about who God is. This type of thinking and consideration about God is necessary, because God's ways are not necessarily natural for mankind. The prophet Isaiah affirms that!

For my thoughts are not your thoughts, neither are your ways my ways, declares the Lord (Isa. 55:8).

Some examples of the differences in the thoughts of mankind and the commandments of God are as follows.

- Mankind hides faults and wrongdoing so others will not think less of it or use its flaws against it. God commands us to confess our sins and ask for forgiveness.
- Mankind uses possessions and talents for personal pleasure. God commands us to use possessions and skills for the good of the kingdom.
- Mankind demands personal rights. God commands us to yield our rights to Him and to find joy in hardship.
- Mankind enjoys the pleasures of sensuality and lust. God tells us that our bodies are living sacrifices to Him and are holy.
- Mankind looks out for itself. God loves and provides for all.

Contemplating things of God is necessary to understand what God wants His people to be and to do. Time spent thinking about God helps us to internalize God's ways and commandments. This meditation is necessary so that God's ways are not foreign to us but are part of us.

Christians are to consider God's ways *all the time.* In the book of Philippians, Paul teaches Christians to meditate on holy things, not earthly things. This instruction emphasizes the importance of our thinking and the subjects of our thinking.

Finally, brethren, whatever things are true, whatever things are noble, whatever things are just, whatever things are pure, whatever things are lovely, whatever things are of good report, if there is any virtue and if there is anything praiseworthy—meditate on these things (Phil. 4:8).

As we meditate on God's precepts and contemplate God's ways, Christians continually look at themselves and their actions compared to God's commandments and ways. This examination is not useful if Christians have not first meditated on God's precepts and contemplated God's ways. This personal examination has several objectives.

- To determine obedience to God's commandments
- To evaluate how well we live by Christ's example
- To consider opportunities to improve our faith
- To assess how we use our opportunities in the kingdom
- To identify our sins and shortcoming
- To appreciate God's blessings in our life

Examine yourselves as to whether you are in the faith. Test yourselves. Do you not know yourselves, that Jesus Christ is in you? (2 Cor. 13:5a).

Another result of our time spent thinking about God is that each person must decide for himself whether he will follow and obey God. God

does not want blind obedience but desires disciples that want to be with Him. He wants followers that have *counted the cost.*

> *Now great multitudes went with Him. And He turned and said to them, "If anyone comes to Me and does not hate his father and mother, wife and children, brothers and sisters, yes, and his own life also, he cannot be My disciple. And whoever does not bear his cross and come after Me cannot be My disciple. For which of you, intending to build a tower, does not sit down first and count the cost, whether he has enough to finish it— lest, after he has laid the foundation, and is not able to finish, all who see it begin to mock him, saying, "This man began to build and was not able to finish"? Or what king, going to make war against another king, does not sit down first and consider whether he is able with ten thousand to meet him who comes against him with twenty thousand? Or else, while the other is still a great way off, he sends a delegation and asks conditions of peace. So likewise, whoever of you does not forsake all that he has cannot be My disciple* (Luke 14:25–33).

Christians actively think about God's commandments to heed His word.

New Testament Example

An excellent example of seeking God, making God's word a part of you, listening and teaching about God, finding joy in God's word, and thinking about God is the story of Philip and the eunuch *(Acts 8:26–40).*

* **Seeking God**—The eunuch was from Ethiopia and not a Jew. However, he had been to Jerusalem to worship. In the first century, many

Gentiles had turned from the idols and immorality of their nation's culture and accepted Judaism as their faith. The eunuch was seeking God.

- **Making God's word a part of you**—The eunuch was reading the book of Isaiah as he was riding in his chariot. Even though the eunuch had business affairs to handle, he spent time in God's word and making God's word a part of his life.

- **Listening and teaching about God**—Philip taught the eunuch about Jesus beginning where the eunuch was reading. The eunuch listened to Phillip and decided to be obedient to the gospel teaching. The cycle of hearing, listening, believing, obeying, and teaching is in the story of Philip and the eunuch.

- **Finding joy in God's word**—The eunuch went on his way rejoicing. He was glad to know the gospel and God's promises. He was free from his nation's idolatry and immorality.

- **Thinking about God**—The eunuch was a man of great authority in Ethiopia. He had studied to understand God's laws and ways. He had evaluated God, God's commandments and characteristics, and the cost of discipleship. He had chosen God and continued to think about God while he was a Christian.

Active commitment to God was required of first century Christians and demonstrated by the eunuch. Active commitment to God is required of Christians today.

Summary

The young man of Psalm 119 teaches Christians today how to be righteous before God. The psalm emphasizes the necessity of time spent in God's word and contemplating God. No Christian can know God and His laws without actively seeking God and heeding His word.

Discussion Questions

1. What do action verbs have to do with living a righteous life?

2. All of us need food, clothing, and shelter. However, we know there are people in the world who do not have those things. Why would Jesus teach that we should not worry about those things?

3. Plenty of spiritual people know the Bible and are unrighteous. How can that be?

4. How can someone teach another about the gospel without excellent knowledge of the Bible?

5. How can someone who is not a good speaker teach the gospel?

6. How can someone find joy in the gospel when the economy has crashed or the person has a fatal illness?

7. Is it sinful to have earthly assets, such as insurance, retirement plans, or savings accounts? Why or why not.

8. What are some additional objectives of our personal examination that the author does not list?

9. Why does the author insist that a person cannot effectively examine themselves without first meditating on God's laws and His ways?

10. What is the cost of being a follower of God today?

11.   Why is "spirituality" not enough for a Christian today?

12.   How are the young man of Psalm 119 and the eunuch of Acts 8 similar? Can you name any differences?

The Bible and Science

Do not hide Your commandments from me (Ps. 119:19b).

Forever, O Lord, Your word is settled in heaven (Ps. 119:89).

Lesson 4: The Bible and Science

God is there for those who seek Him. The writer of Psalm 119 knew this. He implored God not to hide His commandments from him. All of us know atheists, agnostics, and people too unconcerned to search for God. They believe science explains all they need to know.

Most of today's world live comfortable lives with electricity, indoor plumbing, cell phones, grocery stores, and a closet full of clothes. We are not surprised by the weather as our forecasters predict it days in advance with electronic updates at any time. Our scientists use microscopes to study tiny organisms and telescopes to examine the stars. We have teams in submersibles learning about the ocean floor and teams in space stations exploring outer space.

Today science is integrated into our daily lives. We overlook scientific concepts and ideas that were revolutionary within the last hundred years. Our recent ancestors used horses and wagons for travel, a mule to plow, and an outhouse for a bathroom. There were diseases, such as polio and measles, that struck both the rich and poor. We humans have become so comfortable with science and technology that we have forgotten that God made it.

We overlook the fact that God made our world and our universe, along with other planets and other galaxies. He made science and all the laws and principles of it. Throughout the Bible, there are references to science that were unknown at the time of the writing. We just read through those lines because we are familiar with the scientific concept or are not thinking about what the verse is saying. We forget the author had no idea of the technical facts or theory within the text. The author is writing what God told him to write.

The book of Job is full of "scientific" facts. However, Job is not the only Old Testament book with modern-day science in them. Let's look at some texts and discover what scientific principles were written there by people hundreds and thousands of years before "scientists" discovered those same principles. Today, these ideas are so common that we do not appreciate that God told them to us long before scientists discovered them.

Photosynthesis

He grows green in the sun, and his branches spread out in his garden (Job 8:16).

People have always observed growing plants in sunlight. Even our kindergarten children have seen that! However, humankind has not always understood how growing plants and sunlight worked. Photosynthesis is the name of the process a plant uses to convert sunlight into energy.

There are records of studies of plants from thousands of years ago. Early botanical studies have been found in ancient texts from India dating back to before 1100 BC and in works from China dated before 221 BC. Serious studies of photosynthesis began in the late 1700s. However, the overall photosynthetic equation was not known until the 19th century.

A Spherical Earth Suspended in an Expanding Space

He stretches out the north over empty space; He hangs the earth on nothing (Job 26:7).

It is He who sits above the circle of the earth, and its inhabitants are like grasshoppers, Who stretches out the heavens like a curtain, And spreads them out like a tent to dwell in (Isa. 40:22).

The One who builds His upper chambers in the heavens And has founded His vaulted dome over the earth, He who calls for the waters of the sea And pours them out on the face of the earth, The Lord is His name (Amon 9:6, NASB).

The early Egyptians thought the world was a disc floating in the ocean. The Israelites added a dome to this idea to hold up the sun and stars. In Greek mythology, Altas held the heavens and earth apart. Chinese mythology proposed that the world is the back of a turtle and the turtle's shell has markings of heaven and earth and the roof of the universe.

In the Middle Ages of European history, men began to understand that the earth was a sphere that hung in space on nothing. Today we know that the galaxy continues to expand, and the distance between galaxies continues to increase (Edwin Hubble cosmological theory).

Weight of Wind

To establish a weight for the wind, and apportion the waters by measure (Job 28:25).

The ancients had many ideas about the origin of wind without understanding our atmosphere at all. For example, the Norse had a god named Hræsvelgr. Hræsvelgr had giant eagle's wings and sat at the north end of heaven. Winds originated when he spread his wings for flight.

Atmospheric pressure is the total weight of the air above the unit area at the point where the pressure is measured. Thus, air pressure varies with location and weather. The weight of the wind is measured in pascals or standard atmospheres. A pascal is a unit of measurement named after Blaise Pascal (who lived in the 15th century). to quantify the atmosphere's weight or pressure. A standard atmosphere is "a unit of pressure defined as 101325 Pa and is approximately equal to earth's atmospheric pressure at sea level."

Ocean Springs

Have you entered the springs of the sea? Or have you walked in search of the depths? (Job 38:16).

God asked Job whether he had searched the ocean's bottom. Of course, Job could not do that, nor could he appreciate the ocean springs and deep recesses.

Before 1873, people thought the seashore was a shallow, sandy extension from one continent to another. In 1873, British scientists discovered an ocean trench that was 5.5 miles deep in the ocean. Later, scientists found other ocean trenches. Neither Job nor scientists have not walked these depths, but scientists researched them with submersible tools.

Scientists did not find ocean springs until 1977. The first one found was 8,000 feet under the ocean off the coast of Ecuador. Ocean springs are geothermal vents where magma erupts to form new oceanic crust.

The author of Job had not seen either of these!

The Colors of Light

By what way is light parted, Or the east wind scattered over the earth? (Job 38:24).

Rainbows are refracted light and a symbol of a promise of God. Noah saw a rainbow without understanding what he was seeing. A rainbow is a white light scattered into seven colors. Noah saw red, orange, yellow, green, cyan, blue, and violet colors. Only God can separate white light into all these colors and then put them back into one white light.

Movement of Stars

Can you bind the cluster of the Pleiades, or loose the belt of Orion? Can you bring out Mazzaroth in its season? Or can you guide the Great Bear with its cubs? (Job 38:31–32).

We see the constellations that move across the sky with the rotation of the earth. As the earth turns, constellations rise and set similar to the sun. The ancients studied these movements and charted them. Stonehenge (English ruins) and Chichen Itza (Mayan ruins) may be monuments of these studies.

Today we know the constellations also move through space. Stars travel in their separate orbits through the Milky Way galaxy. Edmond Halley discovered the stars' movement almost 300 years ago by comparing current star positions with 1,600-year-old Greek documents.

Over time, the appearance of all the constellations will change. For example, the stars of the Great Bear constellation are moving. The star at the end of the handle and the one at the far tip of the bowl move in the opposite direction from the other stars in the constellation. In the future, the handle will appear to be more bent, and the bowl will spread out.

Radio Waves

Can you send out lightnings, that they may go, and say to you, "Here we are!"? (Job 38:35).

Daily we use radio waves to listen to music and newscasts. Our radios play in our cars, our homes, and our offices. Our radio programs keep up with us as we drive in our cars or ride in trains. Radio waves say to us, *"Here we are!"* and speed through the sky at the speed of light.

James Maxwell, in 1867, predicted the related mathematical theory. Talking lightning! How did Job know?

The Stars

As the host of heaven cannot be numbered, nor the sand of the sea measured, so will I multiply the descendants of David My servant and the Levites who minister to Me (Jer. 33:22).

Galileo said, "The Milky Way is nothing else but a mass of innumerable stars planted together in clusters." NASA's Hubble telescope shows innumerable galaxies flung across time and space. Hydrogen in intergalactic space causes these galaxies to make new stars. Expanding galaxies with new stars can only be numbered by God!

Today, we can appreciate the enormity of our Milky Way on a black night. The Hubble telescope has shown more massive galaxies! The enormous spiral galaxy UGC 2885 is 2.5 times wider than our Milky Way and contains ten times as many stars, about 1 trillion. Jeremiah could not have known how true verse 22 is.

Entropy

For the heavens will vanish away like smoke, The earth will grow old like a garment, And those who dwell in it will die in like manner (Isa. 51:6b).

The second law of thermodynamics is entropy, or the gradual decline of energy and matter into disorder. Here are two examples of this gradual decline involving logs. In both instances, the logs are gone. Isaiah's verse tells us that the world and universe are wearing out just like these logs.

- Solid logs are set on fire. The burned logs become heat, ash, and smoke dispersing throughout the area.
- The logs slowly rot, falling apart, and turn into dirt.

The Sexes

So God created man in His own image; in the image of God He created him; male and female He created them (Gen. 1:27).

He created them male and female, and blessed them and called them Mankind in the day they were created (Gen. 5:2).

All species need a male and a female to reproduce. Neither sex can reproduce without the other. Evolutionists believe species evolved out of a soup of matter. How could a male evolve without a female? Or female without a male? A species cannot survive without both. A male and female of the same species could not have accidentally evolved at the exact moment and in the same place, then mate to continue the species. Not logical at all! The creation story in Genesis is the only logical origination of the sexes. God made them and said, "It was very good" *(Gen. 1:31).*

Blood

For the life of the flesh is in the blood, and I have given it to you upon the altar to make atonement for your souls; for it is the blood that makes atonement for the soul *(Lev. 17:11).*

Blood is life. Man has only begun to understand all the fantastic things that our blood does for us. Blood carries oxygen and nutrients to all the cells in our bodies and takes away the same cells' waste. Our blood fights infection and clots wounds on our bodies. Our blood maintains our body temperature. The components of our blood have exacting properties to perform specific functions to keep our bodies healthy.

Until the late 18th century, bloodletting was common. Blood was removed from a patient to cure or prevent disease, often to the patient's

detriment. Only in the last hundred or so years were the characteristics of our blood realized.

Air Currents

The wind goes toward the south, and turns around to the north; The wind whirls about continually, and comes again on its circuit (Eccl. 1:6).

The preacher is comparing the work of humans to a wind that cannot make up its mind. It blows south one day and north the next day just as mankind runs around here on earth. The wind whirls around and around, just as man's endeavors do.

Ancient mythology has many Air deities to explain the wind. For example, ancient Egypt had several gods for wind and air. This cornucopia of gods would make the wind go every which way!

- Amun, the god of creation and the wind
- Henkhisesui, the god of the east wind
- Ḥutchai, the god of the west wind
- Qebui, the god of the north wind
- Shehbui, the god of the south wind
- Shu, the god of the air

Today meteorologists study the earth's wind. Differences in atmospheric pressure cause wind. Geographic areas (bodies of land and

water), temperature, and other competing winds all influence the wind. Prevalent wind patterns occur globally, such as the Gulf Stream and trade winds.

Paths of the Sea

The birds of the air, and the fish of the sea that pass through the paths of the seas (Ps. 8:8).

The ocean covers seventy-one percent of the planet and holds ninety-seven percent of its water. Ocean currents are located at the ocean surface and in deep water. The ocean has interconnected currents powered by wind, tides, the earth's rotation (Coriolis effect), the sun (solar energy), and water density differences. Deep ocean currents are density-driven and differ from surface currents in scale, speed, and strength.

Density differences in ocean water contribute to a global-scale circulation system, also called the global conveyor belt. The global conveyor belt includes both surface and deep ocean currents circulating the globe in a 1,000-year cycle. In one 1,000-year cycle, a water molecule would travel through the waters of all the major ocean basins: Pacific, Atlantic, Indian, Southern, and the Arctic.

Water Cycle

All the rivers run into the sea, yet the sea is not full; to the place from which the rivers come, there they return again (Eccl. 1:7).

He who builds His layers in the sky, and has founded His strata in the earth; Who calls for the waters of the sea, and pours them out on the face of the earth—The Lord is His name (Amos 9:6).

Ancient people believed land floated on a body of water, and rivers originated under the earth.

Pierre Perrault's studies in the 1600s are fundamental to our current understanding of the water cycle and instrumental in establishing the science of hydrology. The water cycle is the continuous circulation of water within the earth and its atmosphere. The processes within this cycle include evaporation, transpiration, condensation, precipitation, and runoff. The amount of water in the global water cycle is constant. Clouds in the sky, layers of earth, plant and animal life, oceans, rivers, and puddles of rain all are part of the water cycle.

Quarantine

But if the priest examines the scaly sore, and indeed it does not appear deeper than the skin, and there is no black hair in it, then the priest shall isolate the one who has the scale seven days. And on the seventh day the priest shall examine the sore; and indeed if the scale has not spread, and there is no yellow hair in it, and the scale does not appear deeper than the skin, he shall shave himself, but the scale he shall not shave. And the priest shall isolate the one who has the scale another seven days (Lev. 13:31–33).

The COVID–19 pandemic of 2020 taught the world about isolation and quarantine to contain disease. However, the Mosiac Law spelled out the same principles to the Jewish nation. The above verses were guidance for managing leprosy using isolation and quarantine to control the potential spread. This methodology is *thousands* of years older than COVID–19. However, God told His people how to manage infectious diseases by separating the sick from the healthy people.

Summary

Our Bibles tell us remarkable things because our God is an awesome God. God's wonderful creation is spectacular and designed to show His power and might. Paul writes in Romans. God is there for those who choose to see Him.

Because what may be known of God is manifest in them, for God has shown it to them. For since the creation of the world His invisible attributes are clearly seen, being understood by the things that are made, even His eternal power and Godhead, so that they are without excuse (Rom. 1:19–20).

The verses mentioned in this study are not an exhaustive list of biblical "scientific" verses. The author chose these because she could see and explain the current scientific theories mentioned in the verses. Their understanding of science limits Bible students, but our God does not have those limitations.

Sources

Comfort, Ray. *Scientific Facts in the Bible.* Newberry, FL: Bridge-Logos Publishers, 2001.

http://bibleabc.net/l3/has_done/question42b.htm.

https://en.wikipedia.org/wiki/Atmosphere_of_Earth.

https://en.wikipedia.org/wiki/Botany.

https://en.wikipedia.org/wiki/Flat_Earth.

https://en.wikipedia.org/wiki/Hr%C3%A6svelgr.

https://en.wikipedia.org/wiki/Laws_of_thermodynamics.

https://en.wikipedia.org/wiki/List_of_wind_deities.

https://en.wikipedia.org/wiki/Low-pressure_area.

https://en.wikipedia.org/wiki/Photosynthesis.

https://en.wikipedia.org/wiki/Radio_wave.

https://en.wikipedia.org/wiki/Standard_atmosphere_(unit).

https://hubblesite.org/contents/news-releases/2020/news–2020–1?page=2&filterUUID=8a87f02e-e18b–4126–8133–2576f4fdc5e2.

https://learning-center.homesciencetools.com/article/four-elements-science/.

https://spaceplace.nasa.gov/review/dr-marc-space/constellations.html.

https://www.britannica.com/biography/Pierre-Perrault.

https://www.britannica.com/science/water-cycle.

https://www.nationalgeographic.org/media/ocean-currents-and-climate/.

Discussion Questions

1. Is science a religion today?

2. What are your favorite "scientific" verses?

3. How does not understanding the science in a verse limit the reader's understanding of that verse?

4. How do modern lifestyles dull our appreciation of God?

5. How does God use His creation as proof?

God's Support

My soul melts from heaviness. Strengthen me according to Your word
(Ps. 119:28).

Lesson 5: God's Support

The author of Psalm 119 is facing a harsh world. Christians today cope with similarly difficult situations.

COVID–19, a worldwide pandemic, and the Black Lives Matter (BLM) unrest of 2020 are prevalent during this lesson's writing. Distrust and uncertainty are part of daily life. Countries are closed off from each other, and individuals suspect everyone else. Crime and poverty are blasting from news broadcasts, and human trafficking saturates the headlines. Natural disasters batter the country. Wildfires incinerate the western states, and hurricanes drown the eastern states. Tornados tear through both cities and the countryside. Snowstorms overwhelm all else.

How can a Christian know God is in the world when the world is so grim? God knows we need support and encouragement, and He has provided what we need in His word. Joseph's story is an excellent example of God's love and support for His people during hard times—and good times too!

Joseph is the favorite son of the patriarch Jacob and the second youngest of twelve sons *(Gen. 37:3, 35:23)*. Rachel, his mother, died during the birth of his brother, Benjamin *(Gen. 35:18)*. Joseph's life has three phases—spoiled son, slavery and imprisonment, and leader in Egypt, which lead to his status as a Jewish patriarch.

Spoiled Son

Favoritism within Joseph's family did not begin with Jacob. Jacob's father, Isaac, favored Esau over Jacob and his mother, Rebekah, favored Jacob. Isaac and Esau had many common interests related to the outdoors, which probably caused Isaac's partiality. Jacob preferred to stay in the tents, and so, Rebekah loved Jacob more *(Gen. 25:27–28)*.

Isaac's father, Abraham, preferred his second son, Isaac, over his first son, Ishmael. Abraham cast out Ishmael and his mother from his home because of his wife's urging with only bread and a skin of water! God sent an angel to take care of them in the desert to preserve them.

Jacob continued playing favorites in his family, too. Among his wives, he loved Rachel more than Leah *(Gen. 29:30)*. Among his sons, he loved Joseph more than his other sons. Joseph was Rachel's firstborn son and born when Jacob was an older man. Jacob spoiled him! Jacob's prefer-

ence for Joseph was so apparent that all his brothers hated him and could not speak peaceably to him *(Gen. 37:3–4).*

This favoritism had a visual reminder for the brothers as Jacob had given Joseph a coat of many colors—a rare and expensive gift. During these Bible times, most people only had one set of clothes, and dye was very costly. Joseph's unique coat definitely marked him as the special son.

Rachel would have taught Joseph as a young lad, and then Jacob would have taught him as he grew. Evidently, both instructed Joseph about God to establish his faith because of his actions later in life.

However, as a young man, he may have been a little arrogant and had an attitude when he was around his brothers, since he was the favorite son. We all have had interactions with spoiled children! Joseph was the favored son and probably lorded over his older brothers. He was a young man that needed maturity and experience to handle life's situations. Notice the reactions of his brothers to his dream of the sheaves.

And his brothers said to him, "Shall you indeed reign over us? Or shall you indeed have dominion over us?" So they hated him even more for his dreams and for his words (Gen. 37:8).

Of course, they hated the idea of Joseph having any power over them. They were his older brothers! Remember all the seventeen-year-olds that you have known. Could Joseph have had a little attitude? His father is also stunned when told of the next dream of the bowing sun, moon, and stars.

So he told it to his father and his brothers; and his father rebuked him and said to him, "What is this dream that you have dreamed? Shall your mother and I and your brothers indeed come to bow down to the earth before you?" And his brothers envied him, but his father kept the matter in mind (Gen. 37:10–11).

Both dreams shocked the family as they indicated a younger son controlling the father and older brothers. The author is suggesting the favorite son of a wealthy man may also have been a little proud. God has indicated His plans for this young man in these dreams. However, Joseph needed to mature to be the leader in these dreams. The best way to grow and mature is through adversity, and God has a plan for that too.

The youngest boy in a family was usually the family shepherd. As an older son grows up, he moves from shepherd to farmer by sowing, plowing, and harvesting crops with his father. A younger boy then becomes the shepherd. This job passes from older to younger until the last son is the family shepherd. For example, David was the youngest of eight sons and was out with his sheep when Samuel looked at his brothers.

Notice Genesis 37:2 tells us that Joseph is seventeen—plenty old enough for sheepherding. Still, Joseph is at home while the older brothers are out with the sheep at Shechem. Jacob sends Joseph wearing his coat of many colors to check on his brothers. His brothers sell Joseph to passing Ishmaelites as a slave. They bloody Joseph's coat as proof to Jacob that Joseph is dead *(Gen. 37:12–35)*. Joseph is now a slave heading to Egypt. Adversity has landed with both feet on Joseph!

Slavery and Imprisonment

Joseph went from the favorite son of an affluent man to a slave in Egypt! Potiphar, an officer of Pharaoh and captain of the guard, bought Joseph from the Ishmaelites as a house servant. The Bible assures us that *the Lord was with Joseph* and made all Joseph's work prosper. This prosperous activity caused Potiphar to favor and trust Joseph, and he made Joseph overseer of all he had. Joseph's success was part of God's plan, and God blessed all of Potiphar's household *(Gen. 39:1–6)*.

Now it is time for a little more adversity and maturity for Joseph! Potiphar's wife saw handsome Joseph and desired sex with him. Joseph refused and ran away. Mrs. Potiphar is very used to having whatever she wanted from a slave. Joseph's righteous refusal incensed her, and she concocted a lie to cause her husband to become angry with Joseph and get rid of him *(Gen. 39:7–20)*.

Joseph went from the favored slave of a prominent Egyptian to a prisoner in jail. God's support for Joseph is evident in this status adjustment. Potiphar could have killed or sold Joseph, as Joseph was Potiphar's slave. Instead, Joseph is in the royal prison where Potiphar has control of the facility and authority over the keeper of the prison. God had promised to be with His people *(Gen. 12:1–3)*, and His support is evident during Joseph's time in prison.

The Lord was with Joseph and showed him mercy, and He gave him favor in the sight of the keeper of the prison (Gen. 39:21).

The prison keeper put Joseph in charge of all the prisoners and did not supervise Joseph's activities. Again, God made all that Joseph did succeed. During this time, Joseph came into contact with Pharaoh's butler and baker, who were also in prison, interpreted dreams for them, and gave God credit for the interpretations. Joseph predicted the butler would return to his position and asked the butler to remember him. Joseph told the baker that his dream meant he would be hung.

The butler and the baker were notable offices in Pharaoh's royal court. They were probably in the royal prison until Pharaoh investigated a threat against him in which they were the suspects. On his birthday, Pharaoh calls for the butler and baker from the prison. Pharaoh restored the butler to his prestigious position in front of the royal court and hung the baker. His actions served to warn those who opposed him and encourage those who served him.

More adversity came for Joseph, as the butler did not remember Joseph. Joseph remained in prison for crimes that he did not commit! However, God knows there is an appropriate time for Pharaoh to become aware of Joseph. Two years later, Pharaoh has disturbing dreams about cows and upsetting dreams about grain. No one in the palace can tell Pharaoh the meaning of his dreams. Finally, the butler remembers Joseph's dream interpretations and tells Pharaoh about him.

Joseph is brought out of the dungeon, cleaned up, and brought before Pharaoh. God had refined a spoiled boy to gold. Joseph had grown in faith and developed leadership skills while he was Potiphar's slave and a dungeon organizer *(Gen. 40:1–41:14).*

Leader in Egypt

Handsome Joseph had matured into a faithful follower of God and an impressive man. This remarkable person was the individual that God had supported and sharpened through adversity. God had used slavery and imprisonment to develop His tool for saving a family and developing a nation.

Egyptian men shaved not only their face but their entire body. Joseph probably adopted these practices while in Potiphar's house, but would not be able to do this in prison. For dungeon-living Joseph, it would have been like the Academy Award actresses preparing for the red carpet to get dressed to see Pharaoh.

Extraordinary Joseph stood before Pharaoh and interpreted his dreams, giving God all the credit. Seven years of plenty followed by seven years of famine were coming for all nations. Pharaoh believed this interpretation. He appointed Joseph over preparations for the coming famine with power over Egypt's activities, since God had shown him the future. At thirty years of age, Joseph was second in command of the ancient world's most powerful nation *(Gen. 40:15–41:46).* God had used slavery and imprisonment to teach Joseph administration skills, but these thirteen years of training would not have been enough for this enormous task. However, God made Joseph successful again.

Then the seven years of plenty which were in the land of Egypt ended, and the seven years of famine began to come, as Joseph had said. The famine was in all lands, but in all the land of Egypt there was bread. So when all the land of Egypt was famished, the people cried to Pharaoh for bread. Then Pharaoh said to all the Egyptians, "Go to Joseph; whatever he says to you, do." The famine was over all the face of the earth,

and Joseph opened all the storehouses and sold to the Egyptians. And the famine became severe in the land of Egypt. So all countries came to Joseph in Egypt to buy grain, because the famine was severe in all lands (Gen. 41:53–57).

Just as Joseph had given God glory when He interpreted dreams for the butler, baker, and Pharaoh, now he glorified God as he sold Egyptian grain to many nations. After two years, the famine involved the areas where Jacob and his family resided. Jacob had heard about the Egyptian grain and sent the ten older sons to buy some. Joseph would not sell any to his brothers until they brought Benjamin to him. When all brothers are in front of Joseph and very frightened for their lives, Joseph revealed that the second most powerful man in Egypt was their long-lost brother.

Then he said: "I am Joseph your brother, whom you sold into Egypt. But now, do not therefore be grieved or angry with yourselves because you sold me here; for God sent me before you to preserve life. For these two years the famine has been in the land, and there are still five years in which there will be neither plowing nor harvesting. And God sent me before you to preserve a posterity for you in the earth, and to save your lives by a great deliverance. So now it was not you who sent me here, but God; and He has made me a father to Pharaoh, and lord of all his house, and a ruler throughout all the land of Egypt (Gen. 45:4b–8).

God had used the terrible deed done to Joseph by his brothers to preserve Jacob's family! The hairy Canaanites and all shepherds were repulsive to Egyptians, so a separate area of Egypt for Jacob and his family was part of God's support. Jacob and all the people who came to Egypt with him from Canaan now lived in Goshen, an ideal place for livestock. This cultural repulsion and geographical separateness allowed Jacob's family to grow from seventy souls to the nation of Israel and preserved their ethnic and spiritual identity.

God's Support of Joseph and Us

God's love and support do not mean that we will not have problems and adversity in our lives. Life on earth is imperfect and troubled ever since God expelled Adam and Eve from the Garden of Eden *(Gen. 3:14–24)*. Joseph had been a slave and had been in prison. Still, Joseph believed God's promises to Jacob and was faithful to God all his life. His faith was so absolute that God would take the Israelites out of Egypt that he made an oath with them to take his bones as they left Egypt for the Promised Land *(Gen. 50:24–25)*. Joseph knew that God would support and take care of the children of Israel while they were in Egypt and would keep His promises. Yes, God was there for Joseph, but He allowed adversity to refine and mature a spoiled young man.

My eyes fail from searching Your word, saying, "When will You comfort me?" For I have become like a wineskin in smoke, Yet I do not forget Your statutes. How many are the days of Your servant? When will You execute judgment on those who persecute me? The proud have dug pits for me, which is not according to Your law. All Your commandments are faithful; They persecute me wrongfully; Help me! (Ps. 119:82–86).

Let, I pray, Your merciful kindness be for my comfort, According to Your word to Your servant. Let Your tender mercies come to me, that I may live; For Your law is my delight (Ps. 119:76–77).

God's time is not our time. The psalmist in the above verses wanted immediate comfort. Joseph probably did, too, while he spent 13 years as a slave or in prison and governor for nine years before his brothers came to buy grain. The psalmist did ask God "when, " while he searched God's

word and prayed for help. However, the psalmist was confident in God's love and support. He was waiting on God.

God repeatedly assures Christians that He is faithful and will keep His promises. God knows that humans forget His promises, even when He does not. Some examples of this assurance are:

Let us hold fast the confession of our hope without wavering, for He who promised is faithful (Heb. 10:23).

God is faithful, by whom you were called into the fellowship of His Son, Jesus Christ our Lord (1 Cor. 1:9).

No temptation has overtaken you except such as is common to man; but God is faithful, who will not allow you to be tempted beyond what you are able, but with the temptation will also make the way of escape, that you may be able to bear it (1 Cor. 10:13).

He who calls you is faithful, who also will do it (1 Thess. 5:24).

Christians must look to Jacob and Joseph as examples of waiting on God and remaining faithful to God.

By faith Jacob, when he was dying, blessed each of the sons of Joseph, and worshiped, leaning on the top of his staff. By faith Joseph, when he was dying, made mention of the departure of the children of Israel, and gave instructions concerning his bones (Heb. 11:21–22).

God does not promise that Christians will not have troubles here on earth. Christianity is not a charm for riches, good health, and beautiful families as we live here. God promises to be with us during our hard times. Joseph's life proves that we might need some adversity to mature and work in God's kingdom. God is always faithful. We must be faithful to God!

Trust in the Lord with all your heart, and lean not on your own understanding; In all your ways acknowledge Him, And He shall direct your paths (Prov. 3:5–6).

Joseph could not have understood that slavery would make him a better man. His spiritual growth in prison was not a clear path to governorship. Our faith and endurance in hard times refine us and make us a better tool for God. This assurance is one of the best to remember as we Christians work in the kingdom of God. It is part of Jesus's last speech to His disciples and gives personal assurance to us all.

I am with you always, even to the end of the age (Matt. 28:20b).

Summary

God is faithful to keep all His promises. He is with us during our hard times and our good times. God is there to support us and is with us throughout our whole lives. Sometimes God is using our adversity to refine us to be better Christians.

Discussion Questions

1. Why are we more likely to seek God's support when our lives are hard?

2. When is favoritism within a family right?

When is it wrong?

3. Is adversity required to develop maturity?

4. Why did the spoiled son need maturity to become a leader?

5. How did God support Joseph while in Potiphar's household and prison?

6. Why was Joseph successful as a governor in Egypt?

7. How is it significant that Jacob and his family moved to Goshen?

8. How does Joseph's life demonstrate God's support to us today?

9. What is God's time, if it is not the same as our time?

10. What does our faith have to do with God's support of us?

11. What are your favorite verses related to God's faithfulness?

12. Why did God allow the children of Israel to become Egyptian slaves?

Lying

Remove me from the way of lying and grant me Your law graciously… I hate and abhor lying, But I love Your law (Ps. 119:29, 163).

Lesson 6: Lying

The Bible has hundreds of verses about controlling our speech. How many verses from Proverbs or James immediately come to our minds as we begin this lesson? Just listing these verses would take pages! Gossiping, backbiting, murmuring, whispering, muttering, and boasting are all unrighteous and deserving of death.

And even as they did not like to retain God in their knowledge, God gave them over to a debased mind, to do those things which are not fitting; being filled with all unrighteousness, sexual immorality, wickedness, covetousness, maliciousness; full of envy, murder, strife, deceit, evil-mindedness; they are whisperers, backbiters, haters of God, violent,

proud, boasters, inventors of evil things, disobedient to parents, undiscerning, untrustworthy, unloving, unforgiving, unmerciful; who, knowing the righteous judgment of God, that those who practice such things are deserving of death, not only do the same but also approve of those who practice them (Rom. 1:28–32).

Controlling our speech and our tongues is essential, but we will consider only one aspect of speech in this lesson, lying. Lying has been a problem for man throughout time. Man has found a reason to justify lying to both other men and God.

The Garden of Eden

However, a person did not tell the first lie. That honor belongs to the serpent in the Garden of Eden, who distorted God's commandment. Then the serpent said to the woman, "You will not surely die. For God knows that in the day you eat of it, your eyes will be opened, and you will be like God, knowing good and evil" (Gen. 3:4). The serpent perverted God's commandment about the fruit to enhance his personal agenda and made a false commandment of God. Both Adam and Eve allowed this lie to persuade them to disobey God.

The serpent's lie was not elaborate, but it directly contradicts God's commandment not to eat or touch the fruit of the tree of knowledge of good and evil *(Gen. 2:17, 3:3)*. Eve was naïve and listened to the serpent, and Adam listened to his wife. The serpent tricked them into sinning by using their gullibility against them. However, when God called for them in the garden, Adam and Eve hid from God as they knew they were disobedient. Their disobedience and the serpent's lie resulted in curses for the serpent and all humankind and Adam and Eve's expulsion from the Garden of Eden.

Similarly, there are false commandments and doctrines taught today, which may persuade a righteous person into sin. Distorted Scriptures result in a righteous person's destruction. Paul warns the Corinthians that someone can teach a different gospel other than the simple gospel of Christ. Peter also warns Christians about false teachers who distort Scriptures. Eve is not the only one whom lies can deceive!

But I fear, lest somehow, as the serpent deceived Eve by his craftiness, so your minds may be corrupted from the simplicity that is in Christ. For if he who comes preaches another Jesus whom we have not preached, or if you receive a different spirit which you have not received, or a different gospel which you have not accepted—you may well put up with it! (2 Cor. 11:3–4).

But there were also false prophets among the people, even as there will be false teachers among you, who will secretly bring in destructive heresies, even denying the Lord who bought them, and bring on themselves swift destruction. And many will follow their destructive ways, because of whom the way of truth will be blasphemed. By covetousness they will exploit you with deceptive words; for a long time their judgment has not been idle, and their destruction does not slumber (2 Pet. 2:1–3).

If Eve had the serpent, the Jewish people had false prophets, and the early Christians had false teachers, how can we identify false teachers and their lies today? John writes these simple instructions to know when teachings are from God.

Beloved, do not believe every spirit, but test the spirits, whether they are of God; because many false prophets have gone out into the world. By this you know the Spirit of God: Every spirit that confesses that Jesus

Christ has come in the flesh is of God, and every spirit that does not con-
fess that Jesus Christ has come in the flesh is not of God (1 John 4:1–3a).

These spirits are teachers of the gospel. Teachers who do not address God's word as revealed by the Holy Spirit are not from God, but are blaspheming the truth and twisting the Scripture for their profit.

Testing anyone's teaching requires knowledge of the Scriptures! The only way to know the Scriptures is to spend time in the Bible! We must be like the Bereans found in Acts 17, who searched the Scriptures daily to find out whether these things were so.

Then the brethren immediately sent Paul and Silas away by night to
Berea. When they arrived, they went into the synagogue of the Jews.
These were more fair-minded than those in Thessalonica, in that they re-
ceived the word with all readiness, and searched the Scriptures daily to
find out whether these things were so. Therefore many of them believed,
and also not a few of the Greeks, prominent women as well as men (Acts
17:10–12).

How can we decide whether the teacher is spewing lies or preaching truth if we are unfamiliar with God's word? If we determine that the teacher is lying as the serpent did to Eve, we must resist the lie and follow God's commandments. The last verses of 1 John reassure us that we can do just that. When we know God's word and are a Christian, we have confidence in our relationship with Christ and can resist sin.

We know that we are of God, and the whole world lies under the sway
of the wicked one. And we know that the Son of God has come and has
given us an understanding, that we may know Him who is true; and we
are in Him who is true, in His Son Jesus Christ. This is the true God and
eternal life (1 John 5:19–20).

Jacob and Esau

Lying and deception are central themes in the story of Jacob and Esau. Isaac, their father, preferred Esau, the firstborn twin. Rebekah, their mother, preferred Jacob, the younger twin. The custom in those days was to give the primary blessing to the firstborn son, who was Esau. Isaac was old with failing eyesight and wanted to give his blessing to Esau with a ceremonial meal of savory food. Rebekah advised

Jacob with a devious plan to steal Esau's blessing while Esau was hunting game for the meal. She made the savory food and dressed Jacob in Esau's clothes and animal skins on his arms. Jacob only feared the discovery of the deception and was not worried that the trickery was wrong.

> So he went to his father and said, "My father." And he said, "Here I am. Who are you, my son?" Jacob said to his father, "I am Esau your firstborn; I have done just as you told me; please arise, sit and eat of my game, that your soul may bless me." But Isaac said to his son, "How is it that you have found it so quickly, my son?" And he said, "Because the Lord your God brought it to me" *(Gen. 27:18–20).*

Jacob lied to Isaac. His lie led him to blasphemy (speaking sacrilegiously about God). Jacob told Isaac the Lord had brought the game to him, which falsely implicated God in his lies! God certainly had not directed Jacob to lie and Rebekah to guide this deception.

In Old Testament times, the penalty of blasphemy was death *(Lev.24:16).* Frequently, Jesus was accused of blasphemy during His life. Finally, He was unjustly charged with blasphemy and condemned to death: "You have heard the blasphemy! What do you think?" And they all condemned Him to be deserving of death *(Mark 14:64).*

Blasphemy can be a problem in our lives today. We are blaspheming God when we show a lack of reverence for God. Movies and television shows can make a caricature of God for comedic effect. Self-love can replace God's worship and eliminate any sense of His power in our lives. We can use God's name in thoughtless phrases and attribute the good things in our lives to science and humankind. Thoughtlessness allows us to speak sacrilegiously of God. It was easy for Jacob. It is easy for us.

Jacob did not mean to blaspheme God when he was lying to his father. However, one sin led to another sin. Inattentive and careless actions and words often proceed irreverence for holy things. A Christian must always guard her heart and tongue so that only lovely words about God come out of her mouth.

David and Bethsheba

The story of David and Bethsheba should be entitled, *The Story of Many Lies.* The story has blatant lies; lies of omission, and lies of betrayal between David and Uriah, Bathsheba's husband, and one of David's loyal mighty men.

Uriah is away fighting a war for Israel. David uses his authority to have an adulterous relationship with Bathsheba, resulting in pregnancy. David calls Uriah from the front lines of the war and hopes that Uriah will have relations with Bathsheba and believe the baby is his. Loyal Uriah will not enjoy the comforts of home when his men are fighting a war. Then David orders Uriah to be put in the front of a battle and the other soldiers to withdraw from Uriah. Uriah is killed. David marries Bathsheba quickly, so the Israelites will believe the baby is legitimately his child. Oh, the lies of David!

The critical part of this story is the repentance of David *(2 Sam. 12:13).* His remorse for his sins and gladness of God's forgiveness are evident in the penitential psalms he wrote. For example,

> *Blessed is he whose transgression is forgiven, whose sin is covered.*
> *Blessed is the man to whom the Lord does not impute iniquity, and in*

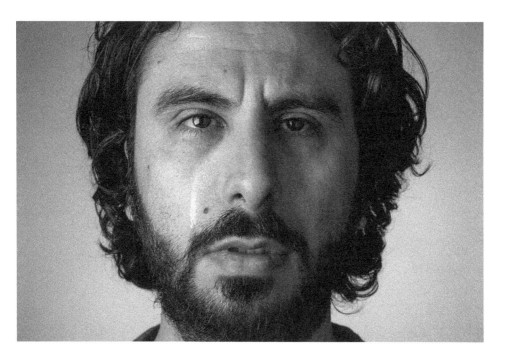

whose spirit there is no deceit. When I kept silent, my bones grew old through my groaning all the day long. For day and night, Your hand was heavy upon me; My vitality was turned into the drought of summer. Selah I acknowledged my sin to You, and my iniquity I have not hidden. I said, "I will confess my transgressions to the Lord, " And You forgave the iniquity of my sin. Selah For this cause everyone who is godly shall pray to you in a time when You may be found; Surely in a flood of great waters, they shall not come near him. You are my hiding place; You shall preserve me from trouble; You shall surround me with songs of deliver-ance. Selah (Ps. 32:1–7).

Remember, O Lord, Your tender mercies and Your lovingkindnesses, For they are from of old. Do not remember the sins of my youth, nor my transgressions; According to Your mercy remember me, For Your good-ness' sake, O Lord (Ps. 25:6–7).

God desires our repentance also. He wants His people to live in righteousness and holiness. David lied about Bathsheba, but his repentance is an example for us. God loved David and He loves us.

Likewise, I say to you, there is joy in the presence of the angels of God over one sinner who repents" (Luke 15:10).

Now I rejoice, not that you were made sorry, but that your sorrow led to repentance. For you were made sorry in a godly manner, that you might suffer loss from us in nothing. For godly sorrow produces repentance leading to salvation, not to be regretted; but the sorrow of the world produces death. For observe this very thing, that you sorrowed in a godly manner: What diligence it produced in you, what clearing of yourselves, what indignation, what fear, what vehement desire, what zeal, what vindication! In all things you proved yourselves to be clear in this matter (2 Cor. 7:9–11).

Acknowledging your sin to yourself is an essential first step. We must know that we have sinned to confess our sins to God. Our sorrowful repentance leads to God's forgiveness and joy in heaven. Train your heart to be like David's, and it will be like God's own heart and do all of God's will *(Acts 13:22)*.

Ananias and Sapphira

The lies of Ananias and Sapphira led to one of saddest events in the New Testament. They had sold some property and gave part of the proceeds to the apostles to support other Christians. They untruthfully told the apostles that they were giving the full value of the property sale. Both Ananias and Sapphira were struck dead for lying to God *(Acts 5:1–11)*.

Ananias and Sapphira were Christians. However, they wanted earthly glory related to their charity and giving to other saints. The property was theirs before the sale, and the proceeds of the sale belonged to them also. It was their choice to donate any or all of it for the saints. The sin was not in the giving but was in the lying. Peter tells Ananias, "You have not lied to men but to God" *(Acts 5:4b)*.

Lying to God is not only a first-century problem, as we can lie to God today. For example, we can take credit for another's work; we can claim more credit than we deserve; we can make promises to God that we do not intend to keep, and we can be as the Pharisees who were righteous on the outside and unclean on the inside.

Woe to you, scribes and Pharisees, hypocrites! For you cleanse the outside of the cup and dish, but inside they are full of extortion and self-indulgence. Blind Pharisee, first cleanse the inside of the cup and dish, that the outside of them may be clean also (Matt. 23:25–26).

God does not want us to be like the Pharisees or Ananias and Sapphira—to appear righteous for earthly glory. He wants His people first to be righteous within their hearts. God wants righteous hearts in His people and is not interested in the recognition they receive here on earth. When the inside of the cup (which represents our character and what we believe and desire), is clean, we have righteous hearts. Our cups are then cleaned on the inside and the outside.

Persons striving for earthly praise are those whose cup is unclean on the inside and shiny on the outside. Worldly honor is their reward. When these people are lying to God's people, they are lying to God. Don't be like these people! Unclean cups are not real righteousness.

Summary

Lying seems like a small, simple sin. However, lying is as unrighteous as any other sin. Simple lies can grow into bigger lies!

False gospels contain lies and distorted truths of God's word. The only way that we can know when someone is teaching a false gospel is to study our Bibles and test the teaching as did the Bereans.

Lying can lead to speaking sacrilegiously of God. Thoughtless words can show irreverence toward God, which is blasphemy.

Lying can snowball into huge, sinful situations. Whether the lie is big or small, God wants our hearts to be repentant. Sorrowful repentance of our sin leads to our salvation and joy in heaven.

Striving for earthly glory can result in lying to God. Real righteousness is when our hearts and our actions are righteous, and we strive for obedience to God.

Discussion Questions

1. Why does Paul put "small" sins and "big" sins together in Romans 1:28–32?

2. How is lying involved in false teaching?

3. God told Rebekah in Genesis 25:23 that the older shall serve the younger. If God foretold that Jacob would have the blessing, did Jacob blaspheme God in his conversation with Isaac?

4. How can we blaspheme God today?

5. Why is David's repentance more important than his lies?

6. How can penitential psalms help us today?

7. Ananias and Sapphira were struck dead for lying to God. Is lying to God an unforgivable sin? Why or why not?

8. How can we prevent being like the Pharisees with a cup that is dirty on the inside?

9. What do Ananias and Sapphira and the Pharisees have in common?

How is that related to lying to God?

Heavenly Treasure

Incline my heart to Your testimonies, and not to covetousness. Turn away my eyes from looking at worthless things and revive me in Your way.… I rejoice at Your word as one who finds great treasure (Ps. 119:36–37, 162).

Lesson 7: Heavenly Treasure

The teacher asked Little Johnny, which was more important today or forever. Little Johnny said, "Today is very nice. I found a lizard under the rock in the creek, the tooth fairy left money under my pillow, and my mom baked my favorite cake."

"That's nice, " said the teacher, who intended to move on to the next student.

"However, " Little Johnny said. "Forever is more important because God is there." Little Johnny is a smart little boy! At a very young age, he knew that spiritual things were more important than earthly things.

During a sermon, preacher John Zellner said, "Home is where our lives are headquartered." He further explained, "We keep our earthly treasures at home, so do we store our spiritual treasures in heaven? Is heaven our spiritual home?" Little Johnny and John Zellner have smart ideas about heavenly treasures.

Commitment to God's Heavenly Treasure

Psalm 119 stresses the value of spiritual treasure so many times. "Your word I have hidden in my heart, that I might not sin against You" *(Ps. 119:11).* The psalmist realizes that we must commit to whatever we treasure, for that is what we value. Someone who is committed to God treasures spiritual things, strives to know God's word, and works to please God. This person hides God's word in his heart so that they will not sin.

Commitment is not just saying the words, "I am committed to God." Webster's Dictionary defines commitment as "the state or an instance of being obligated or emotionally impelled, such as a *commitment* to a cause." Commitments and obligations require time, energy, money, thought, conversation, sacrifice, and protection.

Does God specifically require time, energy, money, thought, conversation, sacrifice, and protections to prove we are committed to Him and His spiritual treasures? Yes, these things are invested by the committed person in their heavenly treasure and are part of our obligation to God.

Time

Time is something that each person has the same amount as everyone else. Sixty seconds are in a minute. Sixty minutes are in an hour. Twenty-four hours are in a day. The difference is how each person uses those seconds, minutes, and days.

Now there was one, Anna, a prophetess, the daughter of Phanuel, of the tribe of Asher. She was of a great age, and had lived with a husband seven years from her virginity; and this woman was a widow of about eighty-four years, who did not depart from the temple, but served God with fastings and prayers night and day. And coming in that instant she gave thanks to the Lord, and spoke of Him to all those who looked for redemption in Jerusalem (Luke 2:36–38).

Anna had dedicated most of her life to God's service. This author is unsure if Anna was 84 years old or had served God in the temple for 84 years. However, her devotion was so exemplary that Luke describes her to his readers. Anna had committed her seconds, minutes, and hours to God and valued heavenly treasure over anything here on earth. God wants the commitment of time from all His followers.

Time is required to read a book, hike a trail, bake a cake, or plant a garden. All these things provide us with things we need during our earthly lives. A Christian must guard her priorities so that earthly activities with earthly gains do not absorb all her time.

To do the things that God commands of us does require time. Study, prayer, fellowship, evangelism, and service to others require time but enrich us with spiritual wealth.

Energy

Energy and effort are required to serve God and obtain our heavenly treasure. Paul is a wonderful example of these qualities with his zeal for service to God. He was active in persecuting the first-century Christians before he met Jesus on the road to Damascus. He was just as zealous to spread the gospel message after that meeting. Paul preached during three missionary journeys and survived beatings, shipwreck, death threats, and other rage-provoked incidents caused by his preaching. He found evangelistic opportunities within Caesar's household during his imprisonment.

Paul spent all his energies to tell all who would listen about God and His heavenly treasures. Even at the end of his life, Paul did not regret spending his life in God's service. In his letter to the Philippians, Paul wrote:

Yes, and if I am being poured out as a drink offering on the sacrifice and service of your faith, I am glad and rejoice with you all (Phil. 2:17).

Paul knew faith and commitment required work and energy. Trust in God's heavenly treasure compels the believer to put that belief into action, just as Paul did. Working in God's kingdom requires energy from each Christian and is no less than God expects.

Money

A contemporary saying for this section is "put your money where your mouth is." Someone who is genuinely committed to their beliefs would have no problem putting this saying into action. Tabitha, who lived in Joppa during the first century, had no problem spending money to support her faith and provided clothes to widows in Joppa. Tabitha put her money where her mouth was.

At Joppa there was a certain disciple named Tabitha, which is translated Dorcas. This woman was full of good works and charitable deeds which she did. . . Then Peter arose and went with them. When he had come, they brought him to the upper room. And all the widows stood by him weeping, showing the tunics and garments which Dorcas had made while she was with them (Acts 9:36, 39).

During Bible times, persons often had one set of clothes and measured wealth in clothes. For example, Samson bet thirty sets of clothes against his wedding guests to solve his riddle (Judg. 14:12). A cloak given as collateral for a loan had to be returned at night to use as a sleep cover (Exod. 22:26). Clothes were expensive!

The expense makes Tabitha's service and charity to the Joppa widows so much more impressive. She used her money to buy the necessary materials to sew the garments. Clearly, Tabitha had the money. She could have purchased necessities and luxuries for herself with that money. However, Tabitha knew that God wanted His people to be taken care of and, through Tabitha, widows had the clothes they needed. The clothes that Tabitha made and the money that she spent show her commitment to her spiritual treasures.

Thought

No one can be genuinely committed to God without thinking about God's word. Thinking and study develop knowledge of God. A person professing faith in God without any thoughts about God is like a leaf floating in a pond. The leaf goes wherever the current takes it without any direction of its own. God wants His people to be purposeful and thoughtful in their service to Him.

Acts 8:26–40 gives us an example of someone who puts thought into their faith—the Ethiopian eunuch. The eunuch had been to Jerusalem to worship and was reading Isaiah to learn more about his faith. He was reading and thinking to understand God's word better. After Philip

joined him, he considered Philip's preaching and concluded that baptism was necessary.

This story of the eunuch shows that faith requires ongoing study and thought. We cannot know what we believe if we do not commit to learning and thinking about God.

Conversation

Our commitment to and faith in God must guide our communication with others. For example, profanity cannot color our speech. Our banter cannot contain complaining and gossiping. We will often discuss politics, the weather, our jobs, and our families. However, our discussions must reflect godly values.

Our daily lives provide opportunities to speak of God, and we must learn to recognize those opportunities. The author worships with a gentleman who must recognize every opportunity afforded to him. People frequently come to our assemblies or Bible studies because he has spoken to them about God and Jesus. This man is not a skilled orator, but he talks to others about his faith. His commitment to God is apparent in these conversations and often influences the listener to learn more about God.

Jesus used conversations to teach. Jesus joined two men walking on the road to Emmaus *(Luke 24:13–35)* as they talked about Jesus's crucifixion. The three men continued their conversation as they walked to Emmaus. Jesus used this conversation to teach them how to understand the Scriptures concerning Himself. Jesus reasoned with them so that they concluded that Jesus was the risen Christ.

For two years, Paul and Felix had frequent conversations about Paul's faith in Christ *(Acts 24:24–27)*. Paul's commitment to the gospel was very clear to Felix. Felix seemed to believe Paul; however, he did not obey the gospel during those two years. Paul used every conversation to teach and influence Felix.

Each conversation that we have will not lead to baptism or another opportunity to converse with that person about the gospel. However, when we believe the gospel and are committed to God, we will use our opportunities to speak about our faith.

Sacrifice

Faithfulness to God does not come without sacrifice. God must be first in our lives before any earthly treasure that we possess. The story of the widow and her mites reveals this idea.

And He looked up and saw the rich putting their gifts into the treasury, and He saw also a certain poor widow putting in two mites. So He said, "Truly I say to you that this poor widow has put in more than all; for all these out of their abundance have put in offerings for God, but she out of her poverty put in all the livelihood that she had" (Luke 21:1–4).

Jesus knew others had given more. However, He appreciated the widow's gift because two mites were all she had. Others had given more, but they had kept some for themselves. The widow had no money left after her sacrifice into the temple treasury.

God does not require Christians to give up all their earthly possessions to be committed to their faith. However, He demands that we value Him and trust in His promises over any worldly possession. This demand is evident in the story of Jesus and the rich young ruler.

Now a certain ruler asked Him, saying, "Good Teacher, what shall I do to inherit eternal life?" So Jesus said to him, "Why do you call Me good? No one is good but One, that is, God. You know the commandments: 'Do not commit adultery, ' 'Do not murder, ' 'Do not steal, ' 'Do not bear false witness, ' 'Honor your father and your mother.'" And he said, "All these things I have kept from my youth." So when Jesus heard these things, He said to him, "You still lack one thing. Sell all that you have and distribute to the poor, and you will have treasure in heaven; and come, follow Me." But when he heard this, he became very sorrowful, for he was very rich (Luke 18:18–23).

The rich young ruler valued his earthly wealth over heavenly treasure and was not ready to give up those comforts. He could not be like the widow and sacrifice all he had to follow Jesus.

After the Jews returned to Judah, Haggai chastised them for building houses for themselves and no place for the Lord. He said, "Consider your ways! Go up to the mountains and bring wood and build the temple that I may take pleasure in it and be glorified" *(Hag.1:7–8).* God demands to be first in our lives over our earthly comforts. Our commitment must be to Him and not our wealth and security.

Protection

We protect what we value. We safeguard our money in the bank safe. We care for our children with nutritious food, child-proof medicine bottles, and car seats. Peter cut off Malchus's ear with a sword to defend Jesus *(John 18:10).* Our commitment to God must be as precious to us as our money and our families and must be as guarded. We must protect our hearts and minds from temptation!

Jesus knew that it is hard for us always to guard our faith. We get hungry and tired and distracted. On the night of His betrayal, He left Peter, James, and John to pray and told them to set a watch. Peter, James, and John fell asleep instead. Jesus returned and said, "Simon, are you sleeping? Could you not watch one hour? Watch and pray, lest you enter into temptation. The spirit indeed is willing, but the flesh is weak" *(Mark 14:37b–38).* It is as hard for us to protect our faith from temptation as it was for the disciples.

God Himself is the fence with which we can safeguard our commitment to Him. He holds us in His hand, and nothing can remove us from it. John 10 and Philippians 4 assure us of these facts.

My sheep hear My voice, and I know them, and they follow Me. And I give them eternal life, and they shall never perish; neither shall anyone snatch them out of My hand. My Father, who has given them to Me, is greater than all; and no one is able to snatch them out of My Father's hand (John 10:27–29).

Be anxious for nothing, but in everything by prayer and supplication, with thanksgiving, let your requests be made known to God; and the peace of God, which surpasses all understanding, will guard your hearts and minds through Christ Jesus (Phil. 4:6–7).

The best protection we have is knowing the voice of God and praying to Him!

Earthly and Heavenly Priorities

Often our time on earth is like the seed sown in the thorns: "Now the ones that fell among thorns are those who, when they have heard, go out and are choked with cares, riches, and pleasures of life, and bring no fruit to maturity" *(Luke 8:14).* Earthly concerns are immediate and urgent. Heaven can seem so far away. The way of the seed sown in thorns appears to be the way to live on earth—enjoying the pleasures of life.

Therefore do not worry, saying, "What shall we eat?" or "What shall we drink?" or "What shall we wear?" For after all these things the Gentiles seek. For your heavenly Father knows that you need all these things. But seek first the kingdom of God and His righteousness, and all these things shall be added to you. Therefore do not worry about tomorrow, for tomorrow will worry about its own things. Sufficient for the day is its own trouble (Matt. 6:31–34).

God knows the demands of our earthly lives and promises eternal life with Him for all Christians. Our faith knows that God keeps all His promises and puts God before all worldly matters. Seeking God first and praying to Him frequently help us turn our eyes away from worthless things and revive us in God's way.

Discussion Questions

1. Must we dedicate all our time as Anna did to have a real commitment to heavenly treasure? Why or why not?

2. What is your favorite example of Paul's commitment to God?

3. How can we use our money, like Tabitha, to serve God?

4. How can we direct our thoughts to God throughout the day?

5. How is continuing to study part of thinking about God?

6. How can our conversations influence others to accept the gospel? Or not?

7. What sacrifices does God expect of us today?

8. Why did Jesus tell the rich young ruler that he had to give up his wealth to follow Him?

9. How can we protect our faith in God?

10. Why is it hard to put God before our earthly concerns?

Hope and Trust

Let Your mercies come also to me, O Lord—Your salvation according to Your word. So shall I have an answer for him who reproaches me, For I trust in Your word And take not the word of truth utterly out of my mouth, For I have hoped in Your ordinances (Ps. 119:41–43).

Lesson 8: Hope and Trust

COVID–19 is rampant at the time of writing this lesson, and the world has shut down. Hope and trust in God become very important when threats appear to our lifestyles because people see that they are not in charge of the world. Science and technology are not the kings of the universe! Science and technology help to understand and manage the pandemic, but are not sovereign over it. God is sovereign over all!

So did God make this pandemic as He has made disasters in ancient times? We know that he flooded the world and saved Noah *(Gen. 7)*. We know it was God's will for barbaric Babylon to conquer and enslave Judah and most of the known world *(2 Kings 25)*. God caused these catastrophes. However, we also know there were other catastrophes

that he did not create. We know that Elijah witnessed calamities of wind, earthquake, and fire, and God did not cause any of those *(1 Kings 19: 11–12).* We know Job lost his family, his property, and his health, and Satan caused those adversities.

Whether God has caused present day calamities is not for us to know, as He has not chosen to reveal that to us. However, God expects His people to trust Him and to have hope for the future, no matter their circumstances.

Hope

By definition, hope is a favorable and confident expectation. We have hope in God when we expect God to keep His promises. This hope is not a frivolous wish, such as a birthday wish, when we blow out the candles on our cake. A Christian cannot wish themselves into heaven!

For example, Paul's hope was part of his defense before Felix when Paul was accused of treason by the Jews. Paul said,

But this I confess to you, that according to the Way which they call a sect, so I worship the God of my fathers, believing all things which are written in the Law and in the Prophets. I have hope in God, which they themselves also accept, that there will be a resurrection of the dead, both of the just and the unjust. This being so, I myself always strive to have a conscience without offense toward God and men (Acts 24:14–16).

Paul's knowledge of God's promises and how God had kept His promises in the past was the basis of his hope. Armed with this knowledge, Paul had a favorable expectation of life after death and a confident expectation of his resurrection after death and standing before God. Hope cannot exist without knowledge and faith.

Paul had not seen heaven, nor had he been resurrected to stand before God. Paul's hope was about unseen things in the future. In his letter to the Romans, Paul reassured them about their hope of glory in heaven and that their perseverance was worth the effort. Paul lived and taught based on his hope.

For we were saved in this hope, but hope that is seen is not hope; for why does one still hope for what he sees? But if we hope for what we do not see, we eagerly wait for it with perseverance (Rom. 8:24–25).

In the opening of his letter to Titus, Paul encouraged Titus with these words related to hope in God and continually encouraged others similarly.

> *Paul, a bondservant of God and an apostle of Jesus Christ, according to the faith of God's elect and the acknowledgment of the truth which accords with godliness, in hope of eternal life which God, who cannot lie, promised before time began* (Titus 1:1–2).

God, who cannot lie, promised us eternal life before time began! This promise is the hope that Paul and Titus had and must be our hope, too. We cannot obtain eternal life with God if it is not something we earnestly hope for and confidently expect to receive. Paul teaches us, "Now hope does not disappoint, because the love of God has been poured out in our hearts by the Holy Spirit who was given to us" (Rom. 5:5).

Trust

The Greek word for trust is also translated as confidence. Trust in God to keep His promises is confidence in God to keep His promises. Trust and confidence are critical elements of a Christian's faith. Christians are confident that Christ came as our Savior to die for our sins and intercedes for us before God. Christian trust is sure that God loves His people, wants them to live with Him in heaven, and is with them here on earth.

The author of Psalm 119 was certain of God: "Your faithfulness endures to all generations." He was confident that God promised to be with Him during all his trials and would keep all His promises throughout eternity.

Trust in God gives us the confidence to approach God, as God has always wanted His people to do. "According to the eternal purpose which He accomplished in Christ Jesus our Lord, in whom we have boldness and access with confidence through faith in Him" *(Eph. 3:11–12).* The psalmist had this type of trust and confidence in Psalm 119.

Often today, people trust in science and technology, forgetting that God created everything. This trust is misplaced when mankind is honoring its human knowledge and not honoring God. God created all the elements of science and the laws governing science. Man can understand God's creation better over time; however, man can never be God.

Not that we are sufficient of ourselves to think of anything as being from ourselves, but our sufficiency is from God (2 Cor. 3:5).

Job maintained a steadfast trust in God during all his trials. However, Job was reminded by God that He had made creation which Job would never fully understand. Job chapter 38 contains some of God's reminders to Job. Job could appreciate and learn about God's creation, but only

God could create it. Job did not put his trust in science and technology, which are man's understanding of God's creation. Job's trust was in a great God, the great I AM.

> *Where were you when I laid the foundations of the earth? Tell Me, if you have understanding. Who determined its measurements? Surely you know! Or who stretched the line upon it? To what were its foundations fastened? Or who laid its cornerstone* (Job 38:4–6).

> *Or who shut in the sea with doors, When it burst forth and issued from the womb; When I made the clouds its garment, and thick darkness its swaddling band; When I fixed My limit for it, and set bars and doors; When I said, "This far you may come, but no farther, And here your proud waves must stop!"* (Job 38:8–10).

> *Have you commanded the morning since your days began, And caused the dawn to know its place, That it might take hold of the ends of the earth, And the wicked be shaken out of it?* (Job 38:12–13).

> *Have you comprehended the breadth of the earth? Tell Me, if you know all this. Where is the way to the dwelling of light? And darkness, where is its place, That you may take it to its territory, That you may know the paths to its home?* (Job 38:18–20).

> *Can you bind the cluster of the Pleiades, or loose the belt of Orion? Can you bring out Mazzaroth in its season? Or can you guide the Great Bear with its cubs? Do you know the ordinances of the heavens? Can you set their dominion over the earth?* (Job 38:31–32).

Our Attitude and Behavior

Our attitude and behavior demonstrate our hope and trust in God but also our lack of it. Demonstrate is a verb denoting action. Strong hope and trust in God are active. A mushroom located in a dark corner reveals activity by visibly growing. We see active hope and trust even when a person is in less than ideal circumstances. Our hope and trust in God can flourish in any situation.

For example, three Israelites named Shadrach, Meshach, and Abed-nego lived in idolatrous Babylon during the reign of King Nebuchadnez-zar (Dan. 3:8–25). These three men were going to be thrown into a fiery furnace and burned alive unless they worshiped a golden image. When asked what god would deliver them from the furnace, they answered boldly.

> *Shadrach, Meshach, and Abed-Nego answered and said to the king, "O Nebuchadnezzar, we have no need to answer you in this matter. If that is the case, our God whom we serve is able to deliver us from the burning fiery furnace, and He will deliver us from your hand, O king. But if not, let it be known to you, O king, that we do not serve your gods, nor will we worship the gold image which you have set up"* (Dan. 3:16–18).

Their hope and trust in God was so *strong* that they would obey and worship God only, no matter their outcome with the king and the furnace. What confidence they had in God! All the verses about Shadrach, Meshach, and Abednego and the fiery furnace reveal their unshakable hope and trust in God. Their attitudes and behaviors made plain that they would only worship Jehovah God. Their hope and trust in God was solid, whether they lived or died by Nebuchadnezzar's hand. For these three men, hope and trust were action verbs.

Prayer Supports Hope and Trust

The writer of Psalm 71 was facing severe misfortune. His prayer, which is a lament, eloquently describes his desperate need and focuses on his hope and trust in God to rescue him.

> *Deliver me, O my God, out of the hand of the wicked, Out of the hand of the unrighteous and cruel man. For You are my hope, O Lord God; You are my trust from my youth. By You I have been upheld from birth; you are He who took me out of my mother's womb. My praise shall be continually of You* (Ps. 71:4–6).

The psalmist is praying that God will remember him during his trouble. His psalm has essential elements of prayer—praise, confession of sin, and requests for our self and others. Throughout Psalm 71:

- He confesses his absolute trust in God.
- He repeatedly asks God to rescue him.
- He praises God.
- He asks for justice.
- He commits to always trust God.

Prayer is how we show our trust in God and ask for God's help. In the Sermon on the Mount, Jesus taught that God knows what we need.

Therefore do not worry, saying, "What shall we eat?" or "What shall we drink?" or "What shall we wear?" For after all these things the Gentiles seek. For your heavenly Father knows that you need all these things. But seek first the kingdom of God and His righteousness, and all these things shall be added to you. Therefore do not worry about tomorrow, for tomorrow will worry about its own things. Sufficient for the day is its own trouble (Matt. 6:31–34).

However, God wants us to know that we need Him. When we pray, we must also trust that God hears and answers prayer. Demonstrate your hope and trust in God with a prayer like this psalmist!

We must trust that God answers prayer for our prayers to be effective. Mindless phrases and expletives are not a prayer. Our prayers reveal the truth of our hearts.

And they were helped against them, and the Hagrites were delivered into their hand, and all who were with them, for they cried out to God in the battle. He heeded their prayer, because they put their trust in Him (1 Chron. 5:20).

Therefore I say to you, whatever things you ask when you pray, believe that you receive them, and you will have them (Mark 11:24).

God listens to the prayers of those who have hope and trust in Him. He wants all His people to pray to Him in the good times and the bad times. Hezekiah prayed for his healing and the defense of Jerusalem against the Assyrian army. God answered his prayer because Hezekiah was His hopeful and trusting servant.

And it happened, before Isaiah had gone out into the middle court, that the word of the Lord came to him, saying, "Return and tell Hezekiah the leader of My people, " Thus says the Lord, the God of David your father: "I have heard your prayer, I have seen your tears; surely I will heal you. On the third day you shall go up to the house of the Lord. And I will add to your days fifteen years. I will deliver you and this city from the hand of the king of Assyria; and I will defend this city for My own sake, and for the sake of My servant David" (2 Kings 20:4–6).

Hezekiah's poor health and the Assyrian threat were bad times. However, Hezekiah's hope and trust in God were evident in the good times and throughout his reign over Judah.

And he did what was right in the sight of the Lord, according to all that his father David had done. He removed the high places and broke the sacred pillars, cut down the wooden image and broke in pieces the bronze serpent that Moses had made; for until those days the children of Israel burned incense to it, and called it Nehushtan. He trusted in the Lord God of Israel, so that after him was none like him among all the kings of Judah, nor who were before him. For he held fast to the Lord; he did not depart from following Him, but kept His commandments, which the Lord had commanded Moses. The Lord was with him; he prospered wherever he went (2 Kings 18:3–7a).

Our Actions Prove Our Hope and Trust Are Real

Hope and trust are inherent characteristics of an individual. Even though our hope and trust in God is an internal part of our being, others can see them through our actions.

Our actions during times of crisis demonstrate our hope and trust in God. Pandemics, poor health, war, financial depressions, and other disasters are trials of our hope and trust. Can we be like Shadrach, Meshach, and Abednego facing the fiery furnace? Like Paul addressing Felix? Or like Hezekiah confronting a grave illness? Our attitudes toward God during hard times must be like the psalmist of Psalm 71—God is with me and will help me.

Good times are also a trial of our hope and trust in God. It is easy to become complacent and forget God when our lives are happy. Comforts are more available to most people today than ever in history. We go to the grocery store for our food without a thought of the required work to produce the food. We walk in our streets without concern of invading armies. Our homes have heat and air conditioning, our closets are full of clothes, and our beds are comfortable. We can forget God in good times.

We must be like David, who loved and praised God in good and bad times. The book of Psalms reveals David's hope and trust in God throughout his life. The following are just a few examples.

I will praise You, O Lord, with my whole heart; I will tell of all Your marvelous works. I will be glad and rejoice in You; I will sing praise to Your name, O Most High (Ps. 9:1–2).

The Lord is King forever and ever; the nations have perished out of His land. Lord, You have heard the desire of the humble; You will prepare their heart; You will cause Your ear to hear, To do justice to the fatherless and the oppressed, That the man of the earth may oppress no more (Ps. 10:16–18).

The Lord is in His holy temple, The Lord's throne is in heaven; His eyes behold, His eyelids test the sons of men. The Lord tests the righteous, but the wicked and the one who loves violence His soul hates. Upon the wicked He will rain coals; Fire and brimstone and a burning wind shall be the portion of their cup. For the Lord is righteous, He loves righteousness His countenance beholds the upright (Ps. 11:4–7).

The words of the Lord are pure words, Like silver tried in a furnace of earth, Purified seven times. You shall keep them, O Lord, You shall preserve them from this generation forever (Ps. 12:6–7).

But I have trusted in Your mercy; My heart shall rejoice in Your salvation. I will sing to the Lord because He has dealt bountifully with me (Ps. 13:5–6).

Hope and trust in God are essential elements of a Christian's faith, just as hope and trust in God have been necessary since God made our world. Our actions demonstrate our hope and trust in God.

Discussion Questions

1. Does God cause the calamities of our modern world?

2. How did Paul obtain his knowledge of God's promises that he preached to Felix?

3. Which comes first—hope, trust, knowledge, or faith in God? Why?

4. How is your hope based on knowledge of and faith in God?

5. Why is it easy to have hope and trust in science over God?

6. How does Job 38 reveal God and His power?

7. How are Shadrach, Meshach, Abednego, and Hezekiah examples to you?

8. Why is prayer important to hope and trust?

9. Why are praises to God part of prayer along with requests for help?

How is praise related to hope and trust?

10. How are hope and trust revealed in our actions today?

11. How is David an example of hope and trust in God?

12. How are hope and trust in God two different qualities?

How are they the same qualities?

Forsaking God

Indignation has taken hold of me, because of the wicked, who forsake Your law… Before I was afflicted I went astray, but now I keep Your word… I have gone astray like a lost sheep; Seek Your servant, for I do not forget Your commandments (Ps. 119:53, 67, 176).

Lesson 9: Forsaking God

In most congregations of Christians, some members have a secret past when they had forsaken God. Some of these members guard their secret to escape being judged by others. Other members tell their personal history to encourage someone else to come back to God. On the other hand, there are "ex-Christians" who see no way back to God and continue their worldly lives. Backsliding from faith in Christ is a real thing!

Throughout time, people have forsaken God, who loves them. The pursuit of money, power, or pleasure and, often, fear of judgment have taken priority over worshiping and obeying God. Forsaking God even happened in the first-century church when the Holy Spirit was so evident among Christians with spiritual gifts. For example, in Paul's second letter to Timothy, we learn of several backsliders.

Be diligent to come to me quickly; for Demas has forsaken me, having loved this present world, and has departed for Thessalonica—Crescens for Galatia, Titus for Dalmatia. Only Luke is with me… Alexander, the coppersmith, did me much harm. May the Lord repay him according to his works. You also must beware of him, for he has greatly resisted our words. At my first defense, no one stood with me, but all forsook me. May it not be charged against them (2 Tim. 4:9–11a, 14–16).

Demas and Alexander the coppersmith prove that forsaking God is not limited to today's Christians. For another example, Egypt had conquered Judah and killed King Josiah. The Judeans had chosen Jehoahaz to succeed Josiah, but Egypt set up Jehoiakim as a puppet king to rule Judea. During this upheaval, the people did not turn to God for help and guidance. They turned to the idols worshiped in the days of Manasseh and Amon *(2 Chron. 35:20–36:8, 2 Kings 23:28–24:6).* In response, Jeremiah writes:

For My people have committed two evils: They have forsaken Me, the fountain of living waters, And hewn themselves cisterns—broken cisterns that can hold no water (Jer. 2:13).

Jeremiah criticized the people of Judah for drinking water from a cistern when fresh spring water was available. A cistern is a tank or reservoir for storing rainwater. Compared to a spring from which fresh groundwater flowed, a cistern leaves much to be desired. The water could get contaminated, or the cistern could leak. Following God is the fresh spring water. Forsaking God is depending on a broken cistern.

New Testament Warnings about Backsliding

The book of Hebrews probably has the most damning warnings about backsliding.

Therefore we must give the more earnest heed to the things we have heard, lest we drift away. For if the word spoken through angels proved steadfast, and every transgression and disobedience received a just reward, how shall we escape if we neglect so great a salvation, which at the first began to be spoken by the Lord, and was confirmed to us by those who heard Him, God also bearing witness both with signs and wonders, with various miracles, and gifts of the Holy Spirit, according to His own will? (Heb. 2:1–4).

Eternal separation from God is our reward for drifting away from God! However, if we do not want to be with God while we live on earth, why would we want to live with Him eternally? When we have known God and His word and choose disobedience, we are drifting away. This abandonment of God is called apostasy.

For if we sin willfully after we have received the knowledge of the truth, there no longer remains a sacrifice for sins, but a certain fearful expectation of judgment, and fiery indignation which will devour the adversaries. Anyone who has rejected Moses's law dies without mercy on the testimony of two or three witnesses. Of how much worse punishment, do you suppose, will he be thought worthy who has trampled the Son of God underfoot, counted the blood of the covenant by which he was sanctified a common thing, and insulted the Spirit of grace? For we know Him who said, "Vengeance is Mine, I will repay, " says the Lord. And again, "The Lord will judge His people." It is a fearful thing to fall into the hands of the living God (Heb. 10:26–31).

Backsliding is a willful sin! Backsliding is turning away from God and returning to worldly pursuits after knowing the word of God. These verses from the book of Hebrew warn us that backsliders cannot escape God's judgment and cannot expect mercy when they have treated Jesus's sacrifice as nothing and insulted God. Verse 31 is an ominous warning to backsliders: " It is a fearful thing to fall into the hands of the living God." Yes, an admonition for all.

Too Bad to Return to God?

At times, a backslider has seen the evil evidence of worldly pursuits and knows God has the righteous way. Solomon is inspired to confirm this in the book of Ecclesiastes when he wrote that worldly pursuits are as grasping for the wind.

I communed with my heart, saying, "Look, I have attained greatness, and have gained more wisdom than all who were before me in Jerusalem. My heart has understood great wisdom and knowledge." And I set my heart to know wisdom and to know madness and folly. I perceived that this also is grasping for the wind (Eccl. 1:16–17).

King Solomon began his reign as a faithful follower of God but later worshiped several pagan idols brought to Jerusalem by his wives, forgetting God. Solomon was a backslider! Hopefully, Solomon's heart re-

turned to God, and the books of Ecclesiastes and Proverbs are evidence of this return.

Evil Manasseh succeeded good King Hezekiah. Immediately after naming Manasseh as the king of Judah, the Bible tells us, that he "did evil in the sight of the Lord, according to the abominations of the nations whom the Lord had cast out before the children of Israel" *(2 Chron. 33:2)*. The following verses of the chapter list many of his abominations.

For he rebuilt the high places which Hezekiah his father had broken down; he raised up altars for the Baals, and made wooden images; and he worshiped all the host of heaven and served them. He also built altars in the house of the Lord, of which the Lord had said, "In Jerusalem shall My name be forever." And he built altars for all the host of heaven in the two courts of the house of the Lord. Also he caused his sons to pass through the fire in the Valley of the Son of Hinnom; he practiced soothsaying, used witchcraft and sorcery, and consulted mediums and spiritists. He did much evil in the sight of the Lord, to provoke Him to anger… So Manasseh seduced Judah and the inhabitants of Jerusalem to do more evil than the nations whom the Lord had destroyed before the children of Israel (vv. 3–6, 9).

How could anyone this evil ever again follow God? Well, King Manasseh did! He realized his necessity for God only after he was defeated and captured by the Babylonians.

Now when he was in affliction, he implored the Lord his God, and humbled himself greatly before the God of his fathers, and prayed to Him; and He received his entreaty, heard his supplication, and brought him back to Jerusalem into his kingdom. Then Manasseh knew that the Lord was God (2 Chron. 33:12–13).

In verse 15 of this chapter, Manasseh took away all the pagan idols, a sign of his genuine repentance. No one can be too bad to return to God!

Solomon and Manasseh realized they must return to God. Persons who die before coming to this realization are without hope of God's mercy. A backslider may read the warnings in Hebrews and not see their way back to God. After all, verse 26 says "there no longer remains a sacrifice for sins," and verse 31 warns of "falling into the hands of a living God." Backsliders may see no way to return to God when they have tunnel vision about the verses from above in Hebrews 10 and these two verses from Matthew 12.

> *Therefore I say to you, every sin and blasphemy will be forgiven men, but the blasphemy against the Spirit will not be forgiven men. Anyone who speaks a word against the Son of Man, it will be forgiven him; but whoever speaks against the Holy Spirit, it will not be forgiven him, either in this age or in the age to come* (Matt. 12:31–32).

An unpardonable sin that God will not forgive! How many backsliders are certain that verse 31 is their damnation? How many "Christians" have judged the backslider and decided the same thing?

In context, Jesus is saying these words to Pharisees, who had rejected Jesus as Christ and were actively seeking to destroy Him. Within prior the verses of chapter 12, the Pharisees had created controversy about the disciples plucking grain on the Sabbath (vv. 1–8), and about Jesus's healing on the Sabbath (vv. 9–13); they had actively plotted against Jesus (vv. 14); and had accused Jesus of following Beelzebub when He cast out demons by the Holy Spirit (vv. 22–30). The Pharisees rejected Jesus's teachings about God's new covenant and the Holy Spirit's work in the

exorcisms. There is and will be no other teaching or offering to save anyone from this rejection. Rejection of the gospel is the unpardonable sin. When a person rejects the way of God, there is no forgiveness for this unrighteousness.

We can return to God by asking His forgiveness and mercy and being obedient for the remainder of our lives. Evil Manasseh humbled himself and implored God for forgiveness from a Babylonian prison *(2 Chron. 33:12).* God, Himself, had told Solomon, "If My people who are called by My name will humble themselves, and pray and seek My face, and turn from their wicked ways, then I will hear from heaven, and will forgive their sin and heal their land" *(2 Chron. 7:14).* God forgave Manasseh *(v. 13)!* Manasseh's actions show the truth of his return to God. For example, he took away idols and their altars, repaired God's altars, offered sacrifices to God, and was an example to his people *(33:14–17).* If evil Manasseh can return to God, a backsliding Christian can, too!

Forgiveness for Backsliders

God always has required faithfulness of His followers and warned them about forgetting

Him. Deuteronomy 6 contains an excellent example of God's attitude about unfaithfulness.

Then beware, lest you forget the Lord who brought you out of the land of Egypt, from the house of bondage. You shall fear the Lord your God and serve Him, and shall take oaths in His name. You shall not go after other gods, the gods of the peoples who are all around you (for the Lord your God is a jealous God among you), lest the anger of the Lord your God be aroused against you and destroy you from the face of the earth *(Deut. 6:12–15).*

What is equally essential is God's attitude toward repentant backsliders. Staying in the Old Testament, consider Leviticus 26 to see that God has always offered opportunities to repent to those who have left God's path.

But if they confess their iniquity and the iniquity of their fathers, with their unfaithfulness in which they were unfaithful to Me, and that they also have walked contrary to Me, and that I also have walked contrary to them and have brought them into the land of their enemies; if their uncircumcised hearts are humbled, and they accept their guilt then I will remember My covenant with Jacob, and My covenant with Isaac and My covenant with Abraham I will remember; I will remember the land. The land also shall be left empty by them, and will enjoy its sabbaths while it lies desolate without them; they will accept their guilt, because they despised My judgments and because their soul abhorred My statutes. Yet for all that, when they are in the land of their enemies, I will not cast them away, nor shall I abhor them, to utterly destroy them and break My covenant with them; for I am the Lord their God. But for their sake I will remember the covenant of their ancestors, whom I brought out of the land of Egypt in the sight of the nations, that I might be their God: I am the Lord (Lev. 26:40–45).

Israel and Judah were exiled into captivity because they frequently broke their covenant with God. However, God always remembered His covenant with Jacob, Isaac, and Abraham. God promised His people that He would never forget them and be their God when they are repentant and return to Him. The last words in this selection of verses are the best assurance ever: "*I am the Lord.*"

Forgiveness for backsliders is not limited to the Old Testament. Two of Jesus's parables teach us that God searches for the lost, including backsliders. In these parables, the woman purposely searches for the lost coin, and the shepherd deliberately searches for his lost sheep. Just as intentionally, God has made a way for backsliders to be part of His flock again. The parables of the lost sheep (Luke 15:4–7) and the lost coin (Luke 15:8–10) also tell us heaven rejoices for repentant souls.

I say to you that likewise there will be more joy in heaven over one sinner who repents than over ninety-nine]just persons who need no repentance (Luke 15:7).

Likewise, I say to you, there is joy in the presence of the angels of God over one sinner who repents (Luke 15:10).

Another parable shows God's attitude of forgiveness to a backsliding brother and His love to both the repentant soul and the soul that had remained faithful. Luke 15:11–31 is the parable of the lost son. The lost

son is our backslider, who repents, and asks the father for a servant's job. The father forgives his son, marks the young man as his son with clothes, signet ring, and shoes, and celebrates the son's repentance and return. The older son is angry that the returning son is back in the family. The father said, "Son, you are always with me, and all that I have is yours. It was right that we should make merry and be glad, for your brother was dead and is alive again, and was lost is found." Both the older, faithful son and the repentant, lost son are sons in this father's heart. God loves both the repentant backslider and the loyal follower, just as this father loved both his sons.

Your Attitude toward Backsliders

Does it make you sad that people aren't faithful to God? It truly bothered the author of Psalm 119.

Rivers of water run down from my eyes, Because men do not keep Your law (Ps. 119:136).

A Christian must first care that a person is not faithful, and then help a repentant Christian. Galatians 6 teaches us to restore a repentant brother into our Christian family and to help him grow in the word of God. The Christian that has not faltered in God's path is not more valuable to God than the repentant one.

> *Brethren, if a man is overtaken in any trespass, you who are spiritual restore such a one in a spirit of gentleness, considering yourself lest you also be tempted. Bear one another's burdens, and so fulfill the law of Christ. For if anyone thinks himself to be something, when he is nothing, he deceives himself* (Gal. 6:1–3).

Just as the father in the parable of the lost son loved both his sons, God loves the penitent backslider and the faithful disciple. How can we not love and accept someone that God loves and accepts? If tears run down from your eyes because someone is a backslider, then help that person find his or her way back to God. Then accept that repentant person as a righteous follower of God, because God does!

Discussion Questions

1. How was it easier or harder to follow God in Old Testament times than to follow God today?

2. Do you think Solomon was a good or evil king? Did Solomon return to God? Why or why not.

3. When someone seeks God's forgiveness in times of duress, as Manasseh did, is their repentance real? Why or why not?

4. How would you help a backslider who thought he or she could not return to God?

5. Is apostasy an unpardonable sin? Does Hebrews 10:26 or Matthew 12:31 teach that God will not forgive those who willfully forsake Him? Why or why not?

6. How is God's forgiveness of Israel and Judea relevant to His forgiveness of Christian backsliders?

7. How are the parables of the lost coin and the lost sheep applicable to repentant backsliders?

8. Why is it hard to accept a repentant backslider into the church family?

What should you and the repentant person do to resolve these issues?

Our Commitment to God

You are my portion, O Lord; I have said that I would keep Your words (Ps. 119:57).

Lesson 10: Our Commitment to God

National Signing Day is exciting for high school athletes as they commit to a collegiate team. A college commits to the student by offering a National Letter of Intent (NLI). to them. The student-athlete commits to the college team by signing the offered NLI. Exciting times for the student and their families and, also, the fans!

The Letter of Intent protects both the student and the team. After signing, the student cannot commit to another college for a year, and the college must honor its scholarship agreement with the student.

Sometimes a student-athlete will not sign an NLI because he or she is waiting on another letter to be offered by a different college or for a better scholarship agreement from the offering college. The college offering the NLI is undoubtedly going to question the student's commitment to its school! On the other hand, after signing an NLI, the school will want the student to stop playing other sports to avoid possible injuries and cease recruiting activities from other schools. The school is only protecting its investment in the student!

God's Commitment to Us

God's commitment to each of us is more powerful than any human can realize. After all, He is God! Our omnipotent, omnipresent, and omniscient God was the great I AM before time existed, and He will be the great I AM after time is finished. However, He chose to love mankind, His creation. He put eternity into our hearts, causing us to yearn for Him. God's love for man is powerful and compelling. The preacher tells us,

He has made everything beautiful in its time. Also He has put eternity in their hearts, except that no one can find out the work that God does from beginning to end (Eccl. 3:11).

God has always wanted mankind to be with Him and has never wavered in this decision. Joshua assured the Israelites of God's unwavering promises after leading them into the Promised Land.

Behold, this day I am going the way of all the earth. And you know in all your hearts and in all your souls that not one thing has failed of all the good things which the Lord your God spoke concerning you. All have come to pass for you; not one word of them has failed (Josh. 23:14).

Matthew 28:20b teaches another powerful promise from God. Jesus is preparing to ascend into heaven, and He tells the apostles, "I am with you always, even to the end of the age." God's commitment to us is so evident in this promise. We are never alone as Jesus is with us!

God has made other promises to us. Some of them are:

And this is the promise that He has promised us—eternal life (1 John 2:25).

If we confess our sins, He is faithful and just to forgive us our sins and to cleanse us from all unrighteousness (1 John 1:9).

However, when He, the Spirit of truth, has come, He will guide you into all truth; for He will not speak on His own authority, but whatever He hears He will speak; and He will tell you things to come (John 16:13).

And my God shall supply all your need according to His riches in glory by Christ Jesus (Phil. 4:19).

For in that He Himself has suffered, being tempted, He is able to aid those who are tempted (Heb. 2:18).

Therefore submit to God. Resist the devil and he will flee from you. Draw near to God and He will draw near to you (Jas. 4:7–8a).

Now, this is the confidence that we have in Him, that if we ask anything according to His will, He hears us (1 John 5:14).

The above is only a short list of God's promises to us. This list includes eternal life, the forgiveness of sins, guidance into all truth, provision for our needs, aid with temptation, a close relationship, and compassion for our prayers. The High and Lofty One who inhabits eternity, whose name is Holy *(Isa. 57:15a),* has made all these promises and more to His creation that He loves. His commitment was evident to Joshua and should be apparent to us.

God's commitment to us is sure, but requires us to be committed to Him.

If you will indeed obey My voice and keep My covenant, then you shall be a special treasure to Me above all people; for all the earth is Mine (Exod. 19:5).

The Christian's NLI

God is so committed to His people that He has made an NLI for us, and it is the New Testament. A testament is a legal will or a statement of fact or worth. It states what a person wishes to leave to his or her heirs in the event of his or her passing. God tells us about His promises in the New Testament, and the Testator has died to make His testament to be in effect.

For where there is a testament, there must also of necessity be the death of the testator. For a testament is in force after men are dead, since it has no power at all while the testator lives. Therefore not even the first covenant was dedicated without blood. For when Moses had spoken every precept to all the people according to the law, he took the blood of calves and goats, with water, scarlet wool, and hyssop, and sprinkled both the book itself and all the people, saying, "This is the blood of the covenant which God has commanded you." Then likewise he sprinkled with blood both the tabernacle and all the vessels of the ministry. And according to the law almost all things are purified with blood, and without shedding of blood there is no remission… so Christ was offered once to bear the sins of many. To those who eagerly wait for Him He will appear a second time, apart from sin, for salvation (Heb. 9:16–22, 28).

Today, our Last Will and Testament is in effect after our deaths. Similarly, Jesus's death put the New Testament into force. The two principle gifts for Christians in this testament are redemption from sin and our inheritance, including all God's promises.

Redemption from sin is necessary to be heirs of God, because God is without sin. Our sin will eternally separate us from God. Sinful people are not heirs of God and all have sinned! "All have sinned and fall short of the glory of God" *(Rom. 3:23).* What a vicious circle! To claim our inheritance of eternal life, we must be sinless. Since all have sinned, we need redemption. The price of our redemption, our freedom from sin, was the death of the testator, Jesus Christ.

1 Peter 1 affirms Jesus paid for our redemption:

Knowing that you were not redeemed with corruptible things, like silver or gold, from your aimless conduct received by tradition from your fathers, but with the precious blood of Christ, as of a lamb without blemish and without spot. He indeed was foreordained before the foundation of the world, but was manifest in these last times for you who through Him believe in God, who raised Him from the dead and gave Him glory, so that your faith and hope are in God (1 Pet. 1:18–21).

We were bought with a price, the testator's blood.

Our inheritance is all the promises of God. The list in the above section mentioned eternal life, the forgiveness of sins, guidance into all truth, provision for our needs, aid with temptation, and a close relationship with God. Indeed God is committed to our NLI. He established His covenant with us before we existed and has kept His promises throughout time. He signed His contract with us with the blood of Jesus and is committed to His promises in it.

National Signing Day

Our Signing Day is the day we are baptized and "sign our NLI" with God. Baptism is how God authorized us to show our commitment to His plan and how we become His heirs.

He who believes and is baptized will be saved; but he who does not believe will be condemned (Mark 16:16).

Then Peter said to them, "Repent, and let every one of you be baptized in the name of Jesus Christ for the remission of sins; and you shall receive the gift of the Holy Spirit (Acts 2:38).

The Spirit Himself bears witness with our spirit that we are children of God, and if children, then heirs—heirs of God and joint heirs with Christ, if indeed we suffer with Him, that we may also be glorified together (Rom. 8:16–17).

He saved us through the washing of regeneration and renewing of the Holy Spirit, whom He poured out on us abundantly through Jesus Christ our Savior, that having been justified by His grace we should become heirs according to the hope of eternal life (Titus 3:5b–7).

Baptism is our signature on our NLI with God. With baptism, we become heirs, and our inheritance includes all of God's promises!

All mankind has been offered an NLI from God. However, not all will accept God's offer with a Signing Day. "For God so loved the world that He gave His only begotten Son, that whoever believes in Him should not perish but have everlasting life" *(John 3:16).* God loves mankind and wants everyone to live with Him in eternity. He has made an offer to everyone!

The decision to decline God's offer is not new. Many disciples left Jesus after seeing all His miracles and listening to His words.

Therefore many of His disciples, when they heard this, said, "This is a hard saying; who can understand it?" … But there are some of you who do not believe." For Jesus knew from the beginning who they were who did not believe, and who would betray Him… From that time many of His disciples went back and walked with Him no more (John 6:60, 64, 66).

To those who choose not to sign, God has also made promises: "For the wages of sin is death, but the gift of God is eternal life in Christ Jesus, our Lord" *(Rom. 6:23).* Death is eternal separation from God. Eternity lasts a long time!

Our Commitment to God

Even though baptism is how we become heirs of God, we must keep our part of the contract. This part involves how we live our life every day. Joshua assured the Israelites of God's unwavering promises. However, Joshua also affirmed his commitment to God in front of all the Israelites too!

And if it seems evil to you to serve the Lord, choose for yourselves this day whom you will serve, whether the gods which your fathers served that were on the other side of the River, or the gods of the Amorites, in whose land you dwell. But as for me and my house, we will serve the Lord (Josh. 24:15).

Our commitment to God must be as strong as Joshua's. His stand was clear and unambiguous, and ours must be the same. We cannot half-heartedly serve God. Jesus taught, "No one can serve two masters; for ei-

ther he will hate the one and love the other, or else he will be loyal to the one and despise the other" *(Matt. 6:24)*. Those committed to God cannot also be committed to worldly masters, such as big houses, riches, and pleasure. God demands to be the first and most significant commitment in our lives. We cannot have two NLIs and be committed to God!

We demonstrate our love and commitment to God when we are obedient to the New Testament commandments.

Jesus answered and said to him, "If anyone loves Me, he will keep My word; and My Father will love him, and We will come to him and make Our home with him. He who does not love Me does not keep My words; and the word which you hear is not Mine but the Father's who sent Me" *(John 14:23–24).*

God has not changed. He has always required obedience from His people:

You shall observe My judgments and keep My ordinances, to walk in them: I am the Lord your God. You shall, therefore, keep My statutes and My judgments, which if a man does, he shall live by them: I am the Lord *(Lev. 18:4–5).*

The writer of Psalm 119 understood that obedience to God was how to show his love and commitment to God: "I have sworn and confirmed that I will keep Your righteous judgments" *(Ps. 119:106).* Both he and Joshua knew how to keep their part of their contract with God.

Keeping and Breaking God's Contract

God has promised more than a college athletic career ever could! Leviticus 26 is a beautiful dialogue of God's promises to the Israelites. The following are some verses telling what He will do when the Israelites keep His contract and what happens when they do not.

If you walk in My statutes and keep My commandments, and perform them, then I will give you rain in its season, the land shall yield its produce, and the trees of the field shall yield their fruit. For I will look on you favorably and make you fruitful, multiply you and confirm My covenant with you. You shall eat the old harvest and clear out the old because of the new. I will set My tabernacle among you, and My soul shall not abhor you. I will walk among you and be your God, and you shall be My people (Lev. 26:3–4, 9–12).

But if you do not obey Me, and do not observe all these command-
ments, and if you despise My statutes, or if your soul abhors My judg-
ments, so that you do not perform all My commandments, but break
My covenant, I will set My face against you, and you shall be defeated
by your enemies. Those who hate you shall reign over you, and you shall
flee when no one pursues you. And after all this, if you do not obey Me,
then I will punish you seven times more for your sins. And if by these
things you are not reformed by Me but walk contrary to Me, then I also
will walk contrary to you, and I will punish you yet seven times for your
sins (Lev. 26:14–15, 17–18, 23–24).

And after all this, if you do not obey Me, but walk contrary to Me, then
I also will walk contrary to you in fury; and I, even I, will chastise you
seven times for your sins (Lev. 26:27–28).

But if they confess their iniquity and the iniquity of their fathers, with
their unfaithfulness in which they were unfaithful to Me, and that they
also have walked contrary to Me, and that I also have walked contrary
to them and have brought them into the land of their enemies; if their
uncircumcised hearts are humbled, and they accept their guilt—then
I will remember My covenant with Jacob and My covenant with Isaac
and My covenant with Abraham, I will remember; for I am the Lord their
God. But for their sake, I will remember the covenant of their ancestors,
whom I brought out of the land of Egypt in the sight of the nations, that
I might be their God: I am the Lord (Lev. 26:40–42, 45).

The collegiate NLI can be voided for so many reasons with no recourse
to set it back in place. God treated the Israelites so much better! He
promised favor when they were obedient to His commandments and
punishment when they broke the contract. However, God promised
opportunities to restore the contract when the Israelites repented and
become obedient again. He would remember His covenant when they
repent and obey. What a loving God!

Our contract with Christ in the New Testament has similar requirements. Christians must keep His commandments. Jesus told Philip, "If
you love Me, keep My commandments" (John 14:15). He summarized to
Philip, "He who has My commandments and keeps them, it is he who
loves Me. And he who loves Me will be loved by My Father, and I will

love him and manifest Myself to him" *(John 14:21).* God, who keeps all His promises, knows and loves Christians who keep His commandments.

However, when we fail to obey a commandment or cease to continue our contract with God at all, God gives us opportunities to repent and restore the contract:

> *The Lord is not slack concerning His promise, as some count slackness, but is longsuffering toward us, not willing that any should perish but that all should come to repentance* (2 Pet. 3:9).

> *Remember therefore from where you have fallen; repent and do the first works, or else I will come to you quickly and remove your lampstand from its place—unless you repent* (Rev. 2:5).

God gives us opportunities to restore our contract with Him. However, although God is forever, our time to repent is not: "And I gave her time to repent of her sexual immorality, and she did not repent" *(Rev. 2:21).* Do not be like that woman Jezebel!

Summary

The psalmist of Psalm 119 understood that our commitment to God was necessary for eternal life. He affirms this many times! For example, "I will never forget Your precepts, for by them You have given me life" *(Ps. 119:93).* He had to know God's requirements to obey the contract: "Oh, how I love Your law! It is my meditation all the day" *(Ps. 119:97).* This psalmist has a lot to teach today's Christians.

God loves and wants everyone to live with Him in eternity. It is our choice whether we accept His offer or not.

Discussion Questions

1. What are your favorite promise verses from God?

2. What promises will God keep that are in the Old Testament?

3. Why did Jesus have to die to be the testator?

4. Does a Christian have preparatory work to get ready for their Signing Day?

5. How does the way that we live show our commitment to God?

6. Why can a Christian not serve God and a worldly master?

7. How can your family or job be important without causing sin?

8. What happens when we break our contract with God?

9. When is it too late to renew our contract with God?

10. Why does God want all humanity to have a contract with Him?

Not Politically Correct

You, through Your commandments, make me wiser than my enemies; For they are ever with me. I have more understanding than all my teachers, For Your testimonies are my meditation. I understand more than the ancients, Because I keep Your precepts (Ps. 119:98–100).

Lesson 11: Not Politically Correct

God's teachings in the Bible are not always politically acceptable positions in today's society. As people become more "enlightened," they depend on their learning to guide their personal decisions and cultural guidelines. Today's society is not the only enlightened people in history. For example, in the time of the Judges, Micah created his own gods and appointed his son as the priest for those gods. The Bible tells us, "In

those days there was no king in Israel; everyone did what was right in his own eyes" *(Judg. 17:6).*

Accepting sin is not unique to people today. The preacher in Ecclesiastes tells us that nothing new under the sun and people doing what they feel is right is not a modern idea. God's teaching about sin is not new, either. God did not tolerate sin in the Garden of Eden, in the time of the patriarchs, or during Jesus's time, and He does not accept it now. God destroyed Sodom and Gomorrah for their sinful nature. Why do we think He will treat us differently?

Man frequently ignores God's constant law and replaces it with a continually changing political stance. Currently, our society cannot decide which public bathroom to use, and parents can determine if their four-year-old boy identifies as a girl. Who would have imagined this confusion even a decade ago?

Sometimes political opinion is contrary to God's law. Christians must abide by God's law even when keeping God's law causes punishment from the civil authorities or personal discomfort within society. Remember, the Sanhedrin had ordered Peter and the other apostles to stop preaching the gospel. Yet, Peter and the other apostles answered and said: "We ought to obey God rather than men" *(Acts 5:29).*

Deceptive Words

There have always been leaders and teachers ready to direct God's people away from righteousness. There were false teachers in the first century, and there are false teachers today. A few modern examples are:

Joseph Smith

- Joseph Smith found buried golden tablets containing the religious history of an ancient American people. These tablets explained that God the Father was once a man who progressed to godhood.

- L. Ron Hubbard taught that everyone is an immortal spirit with unlimited powers over its own universe.

- Mary Baker Eddy wrote that Jesus is not the Christ but a man who displayed the Christ's idea.

Mary Baker Eddy

Peter warned us about these teachers and false prophets. They twist the Scriptures, deny God and Christ, and lead Christians into blasphemy. No one can distort the liberties of Christianity, be indifferent to God's moral requirements, and not suffer the consequences of God's wrath. Peter assures us that God will judge all false teachers!

But there were also false prophets among the people, even as there will be false teachers among you, who will secretly bring in destructive heresies, even denying the Lord who bought them, and bring on themselves swift destruction. And many will follow their destructive ways, because of whom the way of truth will be blasphemed. By covetousness they will exploit you with deceptive words; for a long time their judgment has not been idle, and their destruction does not slumber (2 Pet. 2:1–3).

Paul also clearly warns us about the deception of false teachers in his Corinthian letter. Persons who think immoral living is acceptable because society approves will find God does not have the same opinion. His definition of sin has not changed over time!

Do you not know that the unrighteous will not inherit the kingdom of God? Do not be deceived. Neither fornicators, nor idolaters, nor adulterers, nor homosexuals, nor sodomites, nor thieves, nor covetous, nor drunkards, nor revilers, nor extortioners will inherit the kingdom of God (1 Cor. 6:9–10).

It may be socially and politically correct to accept all political affirmations, cults, and religions; however, false teachers teach unrighteousness.

Emotional Responses

Emotions and excitement of a moment can cause unwise decisions. An agitated crowd can provoke rioting and lawlessness. An exuberant party with music, lights, and friends can make drunkenness and debauchery enjoyable and desirable. Similarly, political decisions often use our emotions to make unrighteousness acceptable. Human emotions can be intense. We can want to do the right thing for a situation, but our decision may not be God's will.

Sometimes it is hard to control our emotions when we are angry. Moses struck the rock instead of speaking to it as God had commanded. Moses was mad at the complaining Israelites and, in the passion of the moment, disobeyed God *(Num. 20:2–12).* For this disobedience, Moses was not allowed to lead the Israelites into the Promised Land.

As Joshua led the Israelites into the Promised Land, God had told them to destroy all the current inhabitants. The Gibeonites tricked the Israelites into believing their country was far away. The Israelites disobeyed God and made a peace treaty with the Gibeonites because of a pleasant meeting with the agreeable Gibeonites *(Josh. 9:1–27).* An enjoyable meal with good conversation and new friends cannot cause us to disobey God!

The Israelite mob's emotion compelled Aaron to build the golden calf because they felt scared and deserted by God. Aaron was the high priest and Moses's second-in-command and knew better *(Exod. 32:1–5)!* The viciousness of a mob is phenomenal and destructive. The Watts riots in 1965 destroyed the community's businesses, killed thirty-four people, and injured about 1,000 more. Recently, a mob attacked the United States Capitol Building, and five have died at the time of this writing. These mobs felt they had valid reasons for their protests but allowed lawlessness to rule them. The anonymity in a mob does not absolve individuals from their role in the mob. Lawlessness is sin. God knew what the Israelites did, and he knew what the Watts rioters did, too.

Our anger, empathy, fear, or reaction to injustice are not reasons to disobey God. Christians must think about their actions and God's admonition to live quiet and peaceable lives. Meek does not mean weak. Remember, Jesus drove the money changers out of the temple!

Some Current Political Examples

Christians live in a constantly changing political world. Enlightenment, technological advances, or the desire for improvement cause change. Christians consider political movements and society's paradigm shifts through God's word. A few examples for class discussion follow.

Abortion

God made us and knew us in the womb. He creates and knows all unborn babies.

But You are He who took Me out of the womb; You made Me trust while on My mother's breasts (Ps. 22:9).

Thus says the Lord who made you And formed you from the womb, who will help you: "Fear not, O Jacob My servant" (Isa. 44:2).

Listen, O coastlands, to Me, And take heed, you peoples from afar! The Lord has called Me from the womb; From the matrix of My mother He has made mention of My name (Isa. 49:1).

Before I formed you in the womb I knew you; Before you were born I sanctified you; I ordained you a prophet to the nations (Jer. 1:5).

One of the most ancient prohibitions is against murder. Cain killed Abel, and God punished him *(Gen. 4:8–12)*. Moses killed the Egyptian and fled the palace to escape Pharoah's punishment *(Exod. 2:11–15)*. The sixth commandment that God wrote on tablets of stone was "You shall not murder" *(Exod. 20:13)*.

Abortion is the murder of an unborn child. An egg and a sperm can meet in a uterus through love, poor planning, or violence. Pregnancy can create problems for the mother due to timing, health, finances, family, marital status, or other reasons. Yes, pregnancy totally involves the mother's body. However, the Bible tells us that we are "fearfully and wonderfully made" *(Ps. 139:14)*. How can we murder someone that God has made?

LBGT (Lesbian, Gay, Bisexual, and Transgender).

Even as the author was drafting this lesson, this acronym was morphing and adding sexual identities! The point is not a politically correct acronym, but to discuss the titled idea of the "movement' in biblical terms.

This section could be entitled *Sexual Sins*. However, LBGT is the current political issue. LBGT is a political movement to gain rights for individuals' sexual preferences and gender identity. A 2017 Gallup poll found 4.5% of adult Americans identify as LBGT (per Google). The United States censuses do not ask about sexual preferences, so a more precise percentage is not readily available.

God made man and woman and said, "It was good." However, over the years following creation, men and women experimented with sex. God was sorry that He had made man *(Gen. 6: 6).* because evil was continually on their minds. The author supposes the evil on everyone's minds included inappropriate sexual relations as all the preceding verses of the chapter dealt with sexual relations. The following chapter tells us of the great flood that killed all earth's people except for righteous Noah and his family.

The Lord told Abraham He would destroy Sodom and Gomorrah "because the outcry against Sodom and Gomorrah is great and because their sin is very grave" *(Gen. 18:20).* Genesis 19 tells of Sodom's sexual depravity when the two angels came to Sodom and Sodom and Gomorrah's destruction because of the evil. Again, the author understands that sexual depravity to be the sin in verse 20.

The New Testament condemns sexual sin many times. A few examples follow.

For out of the heart proceed evil thoughts, murders, adulteries, fornications, thefts, false witness, blasphemies *(Matt. 15:19).*

Do you not know that the unrighteous will not inherit the kingdom of God? Do not be deceived. Neither fornicators, nor idolaters, nor adulterers, nor homosexuals, nor sodomites, nor thieves, nor covetous, nor drunkards, nor revilers, nor extortioners will inherit the kingdom of God *(1 Cor. 6:9–10).*

Lest, when I come again, my God will humble me among you, and I shall mourn for many who have sinned before and have not repented of the uncleanness, fornication, and lewdness which they have practiced *(2 Cor. 12:21).*

Now the works of the flesh are evident, which are: adultery, fornication, uncleanness, lewdness, idolatry, sorcery, hatred, contentions, jealousies, outbursts of wrath, selfish ambitions, dissensions, heresies *(Gal. 5:19–20).*

But fornication and all uncleanness or covetousness, let it not even be named among you, as is fitting for saints; neither filthiness, nor foolish talking, nor coarse jesting, which are not fitting, but rather giving of thanks (Eph. 5:3–4).

Therefore put to death your members which are on the earth: fornication, uncleanness, passion, evil desire, and covetousness, which is idolatry. Because of these things the wrath of God is coming upon the sons of disobedience (Col. 3:5–6).

Sexual sin is not limited to the LBGT community. Christians cannot condone sexual sin that God condemns.

Big Bang and Evolution Theories

The first words in the Bible are, *"In the beginning, God created the heavens and the earth" (Gen. 1:1).* The rest of the chapter describes the orderly manner in which God created our world and all the living things in it. Elementary kids in Sunday school class can often recite what God created on what day, with God resting on the 7th day. Genesis 1 also states that all living things (plants, fish, birds, land animals, and man). all reproduce *"according to their kind."*

Day 1: Light and darkness

Day 2: Clouds and water

Day 3: Dry land and plants

Day 4: Planets and stars

Day 5: Fish and birds

Day 6: Land animals and man

Day 7: God rested

Natural evolution is when plants or animals with more-useful traits, such as more-acute vision or swifter legs, survive better and produce more progeny, causing the preferred characteristic to become more dominant over time. Natural evolution is the basis of plant propagation and animal breeding today. For example, a deer with short legs is quickly caught by predators because it runs slower than other deer. The longer-legged deer will survive and produce more progeny, causing long-legged deer to be dominant. Controlled reproduction of plants and animals improves desirable qualities and has happened for centuries. For example, the corn found by European explorers was more like a heavy grass head than the succulent corn enjoyed today because of the planned propagation of corn by humans.

According to the Big Bang theory, our universe sprang into existence around 13.7 billion years ago. From a black hole of intense gravitational pressure, matter (that came from somewhere) is squeezed into infinite density and heat, which explodes and cools into our universe. This phenomenon is continuing as the expansion and cooling of the universe(s). continue. One common element of the Big Bang theory and creation is that everything has a beginning. Christians agree the universe started with a God-created bang, but not the Big Bang theory. Believing in the fortuitous matter under pressure denies God.

Darwinian evolution theory states that various types of plants, animals, and other living things on earth have their origin in different preexisting types. The distinguishable differences are because of modifications in successive generations over a long time. The orderly evolutionary changes grow into specific plants and animals to the diversity of plant and animal life seen today. For example, a fish developed wings, crawled out of the water, and became a bird. Believing in Darwinian evolution allows man to have no requirement to acknowledge God. He is the supreme being in his earthly kingdom and thankful to have landed on this particular evolutionary path. Humankind can now control its destiny and further evolution with science and technology.

BLM

A Christian should not need a political movement to recognize that a person of color is worth the same as any other race. God does not value a white life more than a black, brown, or yellow person's life. God made all of us bleed red, and all are equal in God's eyes.

Where there is neither Greek nor Jew, circumcised nor uncircumcised, barbarian, Scythian, slave nor free, but Christ is all and in all (Col. 3:11).

The world at the beginning of the gospel era was a socially stratified culture. The idea that anyone in Caesar's household was equal to a galley slave was unheard of! Probably the best example of this equality is in Jesus's followers. This group included fishermen, tax collectors, physicians, tent-makers, leading ladies, prostitutes, soldiers, and slaves. Christianity made all these "equal" individuals into God's children and heirs with Christ. God and Christ do not see the color of a person's skin or their social status. Christians must not either.

The Spirit Himself bears witness with our spirit that we are children of God, and if children, then heirs—heirs of God and joint heirs with Christ, if indeed we suffer with Him, that we may also be glorified together (Rom. 8:16–17).

A political movement should never be necessary to treat all people equally, as God created and values all people. After all, Jesus said, "For whoever does the will of My Father in heaven is My brother and sister and mother" (Matt. 12:50).

Living in Today's World

In the Sermon on the Mount, Jesus tells us to let our lights shine. Christians must live in today's world as an example to others. We cannot be ashamed of our faith, but stand firm in the gospel.

For I am not ashamed of the gospel of Christ, for it is the power of God to salvation for everyone who believes, for the Jew first and also for the Greek. For in it the righteousness of God is revealed from faith to faith; as it is written, "The just I live by faith" (Rom. 1:16–17).

As we live among nonbelievers, we cannot be strident and harsh to condemn all the sin that we see. Remember Jesus and the adulterous woman? He did not blame her in front of the people seeking to stone

her. He told her, "Go and sin no more" *(John 8:2–11).* He did not condone her adultery but advised her to stop sinning. Jesus always condemned sin but loved the sinner. He died on the cross so that sinners had an opportunity for grace. We must also show love for the sinner, but not acceptance of the sin.

> *Take heed to yourself and to the doctrine. Continue in them, for in doing this you will save both yourself and those who hear you (1 Tim. 4:16).*

Paul's advice to Timothy is so applicable today: "Preach the word! Be ready in season and out of season. Convince, rebuke, exhort, with all longsuffering and teaching" *(2 Tim. 4:2).* Christians must be strong in their faith and ready to explain to others about their faith. We never know when our faith is the light for another to the gospel truth.

Lastly, Paul's advice to the Corinthians also applies to us Christians today. In 1 Corinthians 6:9, he reminds them that the unrighteous will not inherit the kingdom of God. However, in verse 11, he says, "*such were some of you.*" None of us are innocent of sin, and all of us need God's grace. Christians are often not politically correct. However, we must love and accept repenting sinners just as Jesus did.

Summary

There is an old saying, "dumber than an ox." Even an ox recognizes his master. Do we recognize God as our master? Christians must know that God is Lord and is supreme over all and rules over any civil government.

Be still, and know that I am God; I will be exalted among the nations, I will be exalted in the earth! (Ps. 46:10).

Discussion Questions

1. What repercussions might a Christian bear for obeying God rather than man?

2. How can deceptive words lead a local congregation into error?

3. Why should a Christian understand the teachings of a cult or religion?

4. When can emotions cause us to sin?

5. How can our emotions help us to make the right decisions as Christians?

6. What should a person do when she has characteristics or preferences associated with the opposite sex? What if the actions discussed in this class cause unhappiness and hardship to that person?

7. How can a Christian reconcile dinosaur fossils with creation?

8. For what reasons might a Christian support a BLM initiative? How would that support look?

9. What "politically correct" situations have you experienced as a Christian? What did you learn?

10. Has the author insulted anyone who disagrees with her by calling them dumb as an ox? Why or why not?

11. The author picked four ideas or movements to discuss more fully. What other ideas or movements would you add to this list?

Our Freewill

I have chosen the way of truth; Your judgments I have laid before me. Accept, I pray, the freewill offerings of my mouth, O Lord, and teach me Your judgments. I have inclined my heart to perform Your statutes for- ever, to the very end. Let Your hand become my help, For I have chosen Your precepts (Ps. 119:30, 108, 112, 173).

Lesson 12: Our Freewill

C. S. Lewis wrote this about free will. "Free will, though it makes evil possible, is also the only thing that makes possible any love or good- ness or joy worth having" (*Mere Christianity,* p. 30). This quote eloquently summarizes why God gave us free will. We can choose to follow Him or not. God values people who choose His path and does not want His people to be like dogs on a leash, with no options but to follow.

The writer of Psalm 119 declares his freewill choice so beautifully! In the few verses picked for this lesson,

- He specifically chose God,

- He plans how to follow God,

- He learns about God,

- He seeks to please God, and

- He looks to God for help.

Choosing to Follow God

Many lessons about freewill use the story when Joshua knew the Israelites' leadership was passing from his hands. Joshua rallied the people, warned them about following false gods, and charged them to serve the Lord.

Now therefore, fear the Lord, serve Him in sincerity and in truth, and put away the gods which your fathers served on the other side of the River and in Egypt. Serve the Lord! And if it seems evil to you to serve the Lord, choose for yourselves this day whom you will serve, whether the gods which your fathers served that were on the other side of the River, or the gods of the Amorites, in whose land you dwell. But as for me and my house, we will serve the Lord (Josh. 24:14–15).

And the people said to Joshua, "No, but we will serve the Lord!" So Joshua said to the people, "You are witnesses against yourselves that you have chosen the Lord for yourselves, to serve Him" (Josh. 24:21–22).

God wants us to choose to follow Him freely and intentionally. Joshua and his house chose the Lord without restraint. It was their choice to make, and God wants our selection to be that way as well. Following God is a deliberate choice–a choice requiring action. Choosing God without intentional efforts is like declaring a college major and then deciding to become a band groupie. The choice of a college major became inconsequential, though it may have seemed important at the time.

Following God is not the same as picking a dinner preference on a menu. This choice defines a lifestyle and requires loyalty, dedication, and faithfulness—even when discipleship is hard and when discipleship is easy. Our God loves all people enough that He does not compel our obedience, but allows us to choose.

Planning to Follow God

The psalmist had laid God's judgments and laws out in his mind and studied them to decide how he would fulfill those requirements. Each of us must consider God's judgments and make our own decisions. Our planning must be like Nehemiah's when he was deciding how to rebuild Jerusalem's walls.

King Artaxerxes had appointed Nehemiah to rebuild the Jerusalem walls, and Nehemiah was in burned-out Jerusalem for three days without telling the residents of his mission. On the third night, he and a few trusted men surveyed the damaged walls to plan what was needed (Neh. 2:1–18).

Nehemiah knew he could not succeed without a purposeful plan. Yes, his plan had modifications when enemies attacked the Israelites while working and when complaints occurred among the Jewish brethren. Nehemiah led the Jews toward completing the walls and gates while thwarting the enemies and resolving issues among the brethren.

Our planning to follow God must be like Nehemiah's plan to rebuild Jerusalem's walls—deliberate and flexible. We must consider our lives and make our plans to follow God's judgments and laws deliberately.

Our strategies must adapt to evolving situations without forgetting the goal of those plans is to follow God. Any idea that does not lead us to God is not the right plan!

Learning about God

None of us can follow God without knowing what God requires from His followers. To do this, we must learn what His judgments and laws entail. We must learn about God!

For example, Manasseh, king of Judah, had done so many abominations that God had declared that He would bring calamity upon Jerusalem and Judah *(2 Kings 21: 11–13)*. Eight verses in chapter 21 are required to summarize Manasseh's abominations! However, 2 Kings 21:9b may be the most chilling: *"Manasseh seduced them to do more evil than the nations whom the Lord had destroyed before the children of Israel."* Under Manasseh's leadership, the Jews had removed God from their lives and forgotten all His laws. After Manasseh's death, Amon ruled for two years, and then Josiah was king of Judah.

Josiah was a righteous king, had chosen to follow God, and had begun repairs to the temple. During these repairs, the Book of the Law was found and brought to Josiah. From the Book of the Law, Josiah learned what God required from His people. Judeans had not met God's requirements for generations! They had not chosen God and had forgotten how to please Him. Using the book, Josiah restored true worship to God *(2 Kings 22–23)*.

Josiah could not have restored true worship as God required without studying and learning from the Book of the Law. Josiah was alarmed at the shortcomings of the Jews in obedience to the Law and knew God was displeased. He immediately began to restore proper worship to God.

We cannot please God without knowing what He wants from us either. All of us must spend time in God's word and then apply it to our lives. Josiah's learning of the Law caused change to the Judeans' daily lives and how they worshiped God. We must also learn how God wants us to worship and to live.

Seeking to Please God

The psalmist in psalm 119 desired to perform God's statutes all his life. He had dedicated his heart to please God with obedience. The first group of exiles to return to Jerusalem understood dedication to pleasing God. This group consisted of more than forty-two thousand people, and their first goal when reaching Jerusalem was to rebuild the temple, for it was God's house. They started the rebuilding process with free will contributions.

Some of the heads of the fathers' houses, when they came to the house of the Lord which is in Jerusalem, offered freely for the house of God, to erect it in its place: According to their ability, they gave to the treasury for the work sixty-one thousand gold drachmas, five thousand minas of silver, and one hundred priestly garments (Ezra 2:68–69).

The seventh month of the Jewish calendar was sacred. Three holy celebrations were observed during that month. Ezra 3:1 tells us that the people came together "as one man."

- The Feast of Trumpets was the first day *(Num. 29:1–6)*.
- The Day of Atonement was the tenth day *(Num. 29:7–11)*.
- The Feast of Tabernacles was the fifteenth day *(Num. 29:12–38)*.

The people had a common desire to worship and please God. Even though they were afraid of enemies within the land, they desired to please God more. Beginning the first day of the seventh month and before they had rebuilt the temple, they freely offered sacrifices to God as directed in His law. These people knew that worshiping God as He directed was pleasing to Him. They also made additional contributions toward rebuilding the temple to please God. The hearts of these returning exiled people wanted to please God more than anything else.

And when the seventh month had come, and the children of Israel were in the cities, the people gathered together as one man to Jerusalem. Then Jeshua the son of Jozadak and his brethren the priests, and Zerubbabel the son of Shealtiel and his brethren, arose and built the altar of the God of Israel, to offer burnt offerings on it, as it is written in the Law of Moses the man of God. Though fear had come upon them because of the people of those countries, they set the altar on its bases; and they offered burnt offerings on it to the Lord, both the morning and evening burnt offerings. They also kept the Feast of Tabernacles, as it is written, and offered the daily burnt offerings in the number required by ordinance for each day. Afterwards they offered the regular burnt offering,

*and those for New Moons and for all the appointed feasts of the Lord
that were consecrated, and those of everyone who willingly offered a
freewill offering to the Lord. From the first day of the seventh month
they began to offer burnt offerings to the Lord, although the foundation
of the temple of the Lord had not been laid. They also gave money to
the masons and the carpenters, and food, drink, and oil to the people of
Sidon and Tyre to bring cedar logs from Lebanon to the sea, to Joppa,
according to the permission which they had from Cyrus king of Persia*
(Ezra 3:1–7).

The book of Ezra tells us that the returning people freely gave of their
means and time to worship God as the Law required and to support the
rebuilding of God's house. The returning Jews pleased God with their
proper worship and obedience to His laws.

We please God with our proper worship and obedience, too. God
gives us a choice. We can worship and obey as He has directed, or we
can choose to do something else. God wants us to "incline our hearts to
perform His statutes to the end of our lives" *(1 Kings 8:58).*

Looking to God for Aid

Psalm 23 is probably the most well-known song of God's care and
protection for His people. The Lord (Shepherd). provides the daily needs,
leadership, security, and love for His followers (sheep).

- The sheep cannot provide for themselves. The shepherd finds the
  green pastures and still water.
- The sheep cannot find their way. The shepherd leads them in paths
  of righteousness and through dark valleys.
- The sheep cannot protect themselves. The shepherd protects them
  with his rod and staff, even his own life.
- The shepherd loves his sheep and provides them with goodness and
  mercy forever.

David looked to God for love and aid all his life. In David's psalms, we
see how David celebrated with God during good times and implored
God's help in bad times. People who choose to dwell in the house of the
Lord know that God will provide them with His love and mercy.

Choosing Not to Follow God

God is a merciful God. He allows us many opportunities to follow Him. As a follow-on to the earlier example of choosing a college major, a person could become disillusioned with a band groupie's life and return to college. If that person lives long enough, they could reevaluate her life, return to college, and work on her life plans utilizing the path of a college degree. However, God is different than college as He accepts everyone that chooses Him. No college acceptance letter is required.

Not attending college has no consequence to our eternal lives—none at all. Not choosing God in our earthly lives has severe consequences in our eternal lives. Joshua assures anyone who decides not to follow God of these consequences.

But Joshua said to the people, "You cannot serve the Lord, for He is a holy God. He is a jealous God; He will not forgive your transgressions nor your sins. If you forsake the Lord and serve foreign gods, then He will turn and do you harm and consume you, after He has done you good" (Josh. 24:19–20).

Only one choice is valid. No other god is real—neither the gods of Egypt or Canaan, nor any god of today. God gives everyone the same option that the Israelites had—follow Him or follow a false god. He hates those who choose to follow any false god. The seriousness of this choice has eternal consequences for each person. No one else can choose for you. We must heed Joshua's example and follow the Lord.

Summary

God has told us how to be pleasing to Him in His word and assured us many times of His love and mercy. He wants us to desire to follow Him without compulsion and the force of His might. God wants His people to be intentional followers who aspire to be with Him and pleasing to Him.

Discussion Questions

1. How do the chosen verses support the idea of our freewill to follow God?

2. Did the Israelites have the freedom to choose God or the Egyptian gods? Why or why not.

3. How is Nehemiah's planning and leadership similar to our planning to follow God?

4. How can we learn how God wants us to worship and live?

5. How can we be pleasing to God today?

6. How does David look to God for help in Psalm 23?

7. Why does God continue to give us the opportunities to choose Him freely?

The Double-Minded

I hate the double-minded, but I love Your law (Ps. 119:113).

Lesson 13: The Double-Minded

The Hebrew word translated as double-minded in the NKJV means "a man of divided mind" and is translated slightly differently in other versions. This particular Hebrew word is only used in this verse. Looking at different translations may help us to understand the psalmist's intention.

- **Amplified Bible, Classic Edition**–I hate the *thoughts of undecided* [in religion], double-minded people, but Your law do I love.

- **Common English Bible**–I hate *fickle people*, but I love your Instruction.

- **Contemporary English Version**–I hate *anyone whose loyalty is divided*, but I love your Law.

- **Easy-to-Read Version**–Lord, I hate *those who are not completely loyal to you*, but I love your teachings.

- **1599 Geneva Bible**–I hate *vain inventions*: but thy Law do I love.

- **GOD'S WORD Translation**–I hate *two-faced people*, but I love your teachings.

- **King James Version**–I hate *vain thoughts*: but thy law do I love.

- **Living Bible**–I hate *those who are undecided whether or not to obey you*; but my choice is clear—I love your law.

- **New American Bible** (Revised Edition).–I hate *every hypocrite;* your law I love.

- **New Century Version**–I hate *disloyal people*, but I love your teachings.

- **New English Translation**–I hate *people with divided loyalties*, but I love your law.

- **New International Reader's Version**–I hate *people who cannot make up their minds*. But I love your law.

- **New Life Version**–I hate *those who have two ways of thinking*, but I love Your Law.

- **Young's Literal Translation**–*Doubting ones* I have hated, And Thy law I have loved.

The psalmist did not have a divided heart and was committed to God and His laws. He hated people who vacillated or were not sure of their faith in God and stated his unwavering faith in God and love of God in this psalm.

Undecided

The classic example of an undecided person is Felix, who reasoned with Paul about righteousness for two years *(Acts 24:24–27)*. Felix even knew the Way from his Jewish wife, Drusilla, even before he met with Paul. Felix waited for "a convenient time" to decide for Christ. The Bible does not tell us if a convenient time for Felix and Drusilla's decision ever happened. Considering his reputation for brutality, Felix probably forgot about Christ after being removed as governor of Judea.

This stubborn refusal to accept Christ's sacrifice and forgiveness is the unpardonable sin of Matthew 12. When a man does not find a convenient time to receive God's grace and acknowledge the power of Christ's blood, God will offer nothing else for that sin.

Therefore I say to you, every sin and blasphemy will be forgiven men, but the blasphemy against the Spirit will not be forgiven men. Anyone who speaks a word against the Son of Man, it will be forgiven him; but whoever speaks against the Holy Spirit, it will not be forgiven him, either in this age or in the age to come *(Matt. 12:31–32)*.

Fickle or Disloyal

Judas is probably the most infamous follower of Jesus. He was one of the chosen twelve apostles, an apostle with a capital A. As part of Jesus's inner circle, Judas spent intimate moments with Jesus as He walked and taught on this earth. However, Judas agreed to betray Jesus to the chief priests for the price of a common slave.

A Christian can be like Judas. No, we cannot sell Him for the price of a slave. But we can be the Christian that is always looking for a better deal. Something like boating on a sunny Sunday or flight schedules in a busy work week can be our thirty pieces of silver. We can put our pleasures or convenience in front of Christ.

We can be disloyal to Jesus because we do not study to understand His word. Some Jewish followers left Jesus because they understood

Him to teach, eating His actual flesh and blood. Jews were forbidden even to taste blood, and the idea of literally eating a man's body was repulsive. In context, Jesus said eternal life was gained by believing He was the bread of life. However, many did not understand the spiritual meaning of the sermon and ceased to follow Jesus *(John 6:32–66)*. They did not put in the work to understand Jesus's teaching and only chose to hear selected phrases.

Our disloyalty and lack of study also allow others to pervert God's word. Hymenaeus and Philetus Incorrectly taught about the resurrection, and those who did not rightly discern the words were led away from Christ *(2 Tim. 2:15–18)*. Christians can be in a "worship" service and tolerate false teaching because they have not studied the Scriptures. Being a light-weight Christian who does not study God's word can lead to fickleness and disloyalty to God.

The cares and pleasures of our daily lives can also cause fickleness and disloyalty to God. In 2 Timothy, Paul writes, "Demas has forsaken me, having loved this present world and has departed for Thessalonica" *(2 Tim. 4:10)*. Demas had been a trusted coworker with Paul, but worldly cares and disillusionment had divided Demas from God. His departure had caused heartache and concern for Paul. However, Paul did not allow Demas's disloyalty to cause a similar disenchantment for Paul. Paul's conviction assures us today: "The Lord stood with me and strengthened me" *(2 Tim. 4:17a)*.

Two-faced, Hypocritical, or Divided Loyalties

God has never approved of two-faced followers. For example, in Jeremiah 7, God told Jeremiah to stand in the temple's gates and denounce the people's sins. The Jewish people had deluded themselves into believing they could do anything, including sin, as long as the temple was in Jerusalem. Jeremiah calls for repentance while the people are coming into the temple. Notice the evils in the following verses are against seven of the Ten Commandments. These people were "religious" on the Sabbath and "worldly" for the rest of the week.

Will you steal, murder, commit adultery, swear falsely, burn incense to Baal, and walk after other gods whom you do not know, and then come

and stand before Me in this house which is called by My name, and say, "We are delivered to do all these abominations?" (Jer. 7:9–10).

God is not blind! Yes, He had promised Canaan to the Israelites, and He had delivered them from Egyptian slavery to live in the land. However, God's promise was not unconditional. Deuteronomy 28 delineates the differences between following God and not following God. Verses 1–14 detail the blessings of obedience, and the rest of the chapter are the curses of disobedience.

Now it shall come to pass, if you diligently obey the voice of the Lord your God, to observe carefully all His commandments which I command you today, that the Lord your God will set you high above all nations of the earth. And all these blessings shall come upon you and overtake you, because you obey the voice of the Lord your God (Deut. 28:1–2).

But it shall come to pass, if you do not obey the voice of the Lord your God, to observe carefully all His commandments and His statutes which I command you today, that all these curses will come upon you and overtake you (Deut. 28:15).

The Jews had to choose. They could obey God and receive His blessings or disobey Him and receive His curses. Jeremiah condemned the

Jews entering the temple for their divided loyalties, and similarly, Moses warned the Israelites of divided loyalties. God did not accept two-faced followers before Christ and does not accept them today.

Christians cannot be two-faced followers. We are either obedient or disobedient to God. Jesus regularly condemned the scribes and Pharisees for this behavior and called them hypocrites. They were super-religious in their public facade and sinful in their thoughts and actions. One of His most picturesque comparisons was white-washed tombs—clean on the outside and full of dead bodies and bones on the inside. A Christian cannot be a hypocrite and also a follower of Christ.

Doubting

In the book of James, there are two sets of verses talking about doubting God. Both groups of verses have a Greek word translated as double-minded (Note "double-minded" is translated from a Hebrew word in Psalm 119). James Coffman wrote that this word was "evidently coined by the author of this epistle, because it is found in no other work prior to this."

*If any of you lacks wisdom, let him ask of God, who gives to all liber-
ally and without reproach, and it will be given to him. But let him ask
in faith, with no doubting, for he who doubts is like a wave of the sea
driven and tossed by the wind. For let not that man suppose that he will
receive anything from the Lord; he is a double-minded man, unstable in
all his ways* (Jas. 1:5–8).

*Draw near to God and He will draw near to you. Cleanse your hands,
you sinners; and purify your hearts, you double-minded* (Jas. 4:8).

James instructs us that we must have faith whenever we pray. Without
faith, we are like a storm-driven sea and tossed about by the wind. Our
faith in God is our most significant obligation, more than our families,
jobs, and other responsibilities. Anyone who doubts God cannot be
stable with other duties in their life when they are weak in the most
important one.

Neither can a Christian draw near to God with doubt in their hearts
and minds. This contradiction is like a pushmi-pullyu—the fictional
creature from the children's story, *Doctor Dolittle,* with a head on both
ends—pushing toward and pulling away from God. God does not accept doubters!

Vain Intentions and Thoughts

Vain Intentions and thoughts are those which are unproductive or
useless. For example, the rich young ruler intended to follow Jesus, but
was too interested in remaining wealthy to do so (Mark 10:17–22). His intentions and thoughts were useless as he did not turn them into action.
The rich young ruler put off following Christ until he got "a round to it,"
but that is not how faith in Christ works.

We can daydream about a lot of things. However, we continue to drift
in our dreams without effort, and none of them becomes a reality. We
cannot go to college unless we apply for entrance and attend classes.
We cannot buy a house unless we save for the down payment and
qualify for a mortgage. Worldly dreams require effort, and Christianity
does too.

*But be doers of the word, and not hearers only, deceiving yourselves. For
if anyone is a hearer of the word and not a doer, he is like a man ob-*

serving his natural face in a mirror; for he observes himself, goes away, and immediately forgets what kind of man he was. But he who looks into the perfect law of liberty and continues in it, and is not a forgetful hearer but a doer of the work, this one will be blessed in what he does (Jas. 1:22–25).

A person cannot be like the rich young ruler by only glancing into the mirror of the perfect law of liberty. A Christian must see her reflection, remove the dirt from her face, and straighten her hair to prepare for the day. This Christian must delve into God's law, remember what God has said, and then do God's work. A Christian is a doer!

Summary

A double-minded person is never a strong Christian, as the world colors her faith more than God's wisdom. Indecision, disloyalty, hypocrisy, doubt, and unproductivity are all characteristics of a weak Christian. The conviction of God's truth demands work, and a strong Christian is a doer of God's word.

Discussion Questions

1. How do you interpret the meaning of "double-minded" in verse 113?

2. When is a "convenient time" too late for salvation?

3. Do you agree that the unpardonable sin is not accepting Christ? Why or why not?

4. How can we protect ourselves against Judas's disloyalty or Demas's disillusionment?

5. How can a Christian today be a hypocrite as the scribes and Pharisees during Jesus's lifetime?

6. How can being a "Sunday Christian" put the church in a bad light? How can we explain that to a non-believer?

7. When can a strong Christian doubt God?

8. How can doubt exist in our prayers?

9. How can we be like a pushmi-pullyu with God?

10. How was the rich young ruler like a person who glances in the mirror?

11. How can we be a doer of God's word?

Justice from God

It is time for You to act, O Lord, for they have regarded Your law as void
(Ps. 119:126).

Lesson 14: Justice from God

The desire for justice is not a new longing for humankind. Unwarranted violence, poverty, sexual slavery, disease, and all unfairness demand justice. Every parent holding her injured child cries, "Why?" Every victim of murder, robbery, and assault yearn for vindication. David implored God for justice in many of his psalms. A reader does not have to read far into the book of Psalms to find examples from David.

Arise, O Lord; Save me, O my God! For You have struck all my enemies on the cheekbone; You have broken the teeth of the ungodly (Ps. 3:7).

How long, O you sons of men, Will you turn my glory to shame? How long will you love worthlessness And seek falsehood? Selah But know

that the Lord has set apart for Himself him who is godly; The Lord will hear when I call to Him (Ps. 4:2–3).

My soul also is greatly troubled; But You, O Lord—how long? Return, O Lord, deliver me! Oh, save me for Your mercies' sake! (Ps. 6:3–4).

How Long?

David asks, "How long?" in Psalm 6. In this particular psalm, David is asking for healing from a severe illness. "Heal me, for my bones are troubled" *(v. 2)*. Like every human, David pleads, "How long?" He is impatient as we are impatient. We want what we want now! There is a similar vignette in Revelation 6.

When He opened the fifth seal, I saw under the altar the souls of those who had been slain for the word of God and for the testimony which they held. And they cried with a loud voice, saying, "How long, O Lord, holy and true, until You judge and avenge our blood on those who dwell on the earth?" Then a white robe was given to each of them; and it was said to them that they should rest a little while longer, until both the number of their fellow servants and their brethren, who would be killed as they were, was completed *(Rev. 6:9–11)*.

The souls under the altar are martyrs slain for their faith in Christ. They are impatient and call out for vengeance for the atrocities committed against them. "How long, O Lord, holy and true, until You judge and avenge our blood on those who dwell on the earth?" These souls want God to judge and convict all who sinned against them. They want justice for their spilled blood!

God's time is not the same as these martyrs' time. They are given a white robe and told to rest a while longer. God was not ready to exact His justice just because the faithful demanded it. The vengeance requested by the souls under the altar is not complete until Revelation 19. God's plan is not our plan.

Old Testament Justice

Many chapters and verses of the first five books of the Old Testament specify penalties for acts of injustice. As harsh as these laws seem to us today, they were very different from primitive laws of the time. Primitive

retributions may have resulted in the death of whole families for per-ceived slights. The Mosaic Law limited punishments with considerations for the original injury or loss. These examples from Exodus 21 have guid-ance for Hebrew slavery, murder, and animal control.

> *And if a man sells his daughter to be a female slave, she shall not go out as the male slaves do. If he takes another wife, he shall not diminish her food, her clothing, and her marriage rights. And if he does not do these three for her, then she shall go out free, without paying money (Exod. 21:7, 10–11).*

> *He who strikes a man so that he dies shall surely be put to death. How-ever, if he did not lie in wait, but God delivered him into his hand, then I will appoint for you a place where he may flee (Exod. 21:12–13).*

> *If men fight, and hurt a woman with child, so that she gives birth prematurely, yet no harm follows, he shall surely be punished accord-ingly as the woman's husband imposes on him; and he shall pay as the judges determine. But if any harm follows, then you shall give life for life, eye for eye, tooth for tooth, hand for hand, foot for foot, burn for burn, wound for wound, stripe for stripe (Exod. 21:22–24).*

If one man's ox hurts another's, so that it dies, then they shall sell the live ox and divide the money from it; and the dead ox they shall also divide. Or if it was known that the ox tended to thrust in time past, and its owner has not kept it confined, he shall surely pay ox for ox, and the dead animal shall be his own (Exod. 21:35–36).

Verse 24 is often quoted when exacting justice: "An eye for an eye, a tooth for a tooth." Leviticus 24:20 and Deuteronomy 19:21 have similar wording. Mosaic Law required that man's justice had to fit the crime or the nature of the injury. An out-of-proportion sentence for a crime was not part of God's law.

For example, an out-of-proportion justice was in the control of royal forests during medieval times. The king claimed large tracts of forests. The king's law declared hunting animals in the royal forests as poaching. Anyone caught faced harsh punishments, from hanging to castration or blinding. A few rabbits for a hungry family versus medieval punishment was not in line with God's law. Medieval kings must not have been students of Old Testament justice and sense of fairness!

An Eye for an Eye

An eye for an eye was an essential concept for Mosaic Law. It was called the law of retaliation and limited the punishment for an offender. However, Jesus gives Christians new guidance for revenge in His Sermon on the Mount.

You have heard that it was said, "An eye for an eye and a tooth for a tooth." But I tell you not to resist an evil person. But whoever slaps you on your right cheek, turn the other to him also. If anyone wants to sue

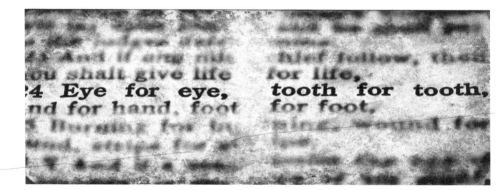

*you and take away your tunic, let him have your cloak also. And who-
ever compels you to go one mile, go with him two. Give to him who asks
you, and from him who wants to borrow from you do not turn away*
(Matt. 5:38–42).

These verses are some of the hardest for an injured Christian. Turn the
other cheek. Do not resist. Go the extra mile. In these few verses, Jesus
indicates a Christian does not retaliate for physical attacks, lawsuits, government demands, and financial requests. Jesus is not telling us to let
everyone injure or steal from us or support evil governmental laws. The
early church certainly did not act in this manner. Maybe the best way to
consider these verses is through Jesus's life and His meekness.

- Jesus left when people attempted to stone Him instead of defend-
  ing Himself or attacking the crowd *(John 8:59).*

- Jesus warned one from the crowd about covetousness when asked
  about forcing a sharing of an inheritance *(Luke 12:13–14).*

- Jesus allowed Himself to be arrested, humiliated, and crucified *(Mark
  14:43–15:41).*

- Jesus told us to pay our taxes *(Matt. 17:24–27).*

Meek is a hard word for us to understand. We often think of meek as
weak, without strength. Wikipedia says this about meekness. Meekness is
an attribute of human nature and behavior, defined as an amalgam of righteousness, inner humility, and patience. Christians are to be submissively
meek as Jesus was, which incorporates the above verses into daily life.

*Therefore, as the elect of God, holy and beloved, put on tender mercies,
kindness, humility, meekness, longsuffering; bearing with one another, and
forgiving one another, if anyone has a complaint against another; even as
Christ forgave you, so you also must do* *(Col. 3:12–13).*

View Matthew 5:38–42 through lenses of New Testament Christians'
actions. These people did what was right before God and gave up their
"rights" for other men. They were not arrogant, loud, or boastful, but had
strength and patience in their righteousness before God.

- Jesus said, "Father, forgive them, for they do not know what they do"
  (Luke 23:34).

- Paul wrote to Timothy. The servant of the Lord must be gentle, apt to teach, patient, in meekness instructing those that oppose them-selves *(2 Tim. 2:24–25)*.

- Simon of Cyrene carried Jesus's cross *(Matt. 27:32)*.

- Barnabas sold his land to support other Christians *(Acts 4:36–37)*.

God's Justice

Man's justice is not God's justice. Christians are not to return evil for evil, but evil for good and live peaceably with all men as much as pos-sible with active goodwill. God does not allow His people to have final justice. He reserves that for Himself.

If it is possible, as much as depends on you, live peaceably with all men. Beloved, do not avenge yourselves, but rather give place to wrath; for it is written, "Vengeance is Mine, I will repay," says the Lord. Therefore "If your enemy is hungry, feed him; If he is thirsty, give him a drink; For in so doing you will heap coals of fire on his head" (Rom. 12:18–20).

God will judge each person by his or her deeds, and no one will escape His justice. This judgment is as sure and certain as any of His promises. Even the most ardent atheist will acknowledge the might and power of God on that day.

But in accordance with your hardness and your impenitent heart you are treasuring up for yourself wrath in the day of wrath and revelation of the righteous judgment of God, who "will render to each one accord-ing to his deeds": eternal life to those who by patient continuance in doing good seek for glory, honor, and immortality; but to those who are self-seeking and do not obey the truth, but obey unrighteousness—in-dignation and wrath, tribulation and anguish, on every soul of man who does evil, of the Jew first and also of the Greek; but glory, honor, and peace to everyone who works what is good, to the Jew first and also to the Greek. For there is no partiality with God (Rom. 2:5–11).

For we shall all stand before the judgment seat of Christ. For it is written: "As I live, says the Lord, Every knee shall bow to Me, And every tongue shall confess to God." So then each of us shall give account of himself to God (Rom. 14:10b–12).

God's Time

We will not have justice for all the sins against us while we live on earth. That was never God's goal. Even the specified punishments under the Old Law were to manage people's passions, not to limit God's judgment. The throne scene of Revelation 20 is a poignant portrayal of God's final judgment to man occurring in God's time.

Then I saw a great white throne and Him who sat on it, from whose face the earth and the heaven fled away. And there was found no place for them. And I saw the dead, small and great, standing before God, and books were opened. And another book was opened, which is the Book of Life. And the dead were judged according to their works, by the things which were written in the books. The sea gave up the dead who were in it, and Death and Hades delivered up the dead who were in them. And they were judged, each one according to his works. Then Death and Hades were cast into the lake of fire. This is the second death. And anyone not found written in the Book of Life was cast into the lake of fire (Rev. 20:11–15).

The psalmist of Psalm 119 cried to God for vengeance for those who had done him wrong: "The proud have dug pits for me, Which is not according to Your law. All Your commandments are faithful; They perse-

cute me wrongfully; Help me!" *(Ps. 119:85–86).* **The psalmist is focused on his life at the time, not his eternal life.**

It is not sinful to pray to God for vengeance and help in our hard times. However, God will decide when to punish, not man. In John's vision, God told him,

> *It is done! I am the Alpha and the Omega, the Beginning and the End. I will give of the fountain of the water of life freely to him who thirsts. He who overcomes shall inherit all things, and I will be his God and he shall be My son. But the cowardly, unbelieving, abominable, murderers, sexually immoral, sorcerers, idolaters, and all liars shall have their part in the lake which burns with fire and brimstone, which is the second death* (Rev. 21: 6–8).

God is the great *I Am* who will judge all people. It is inevitable.

Summary

God assures Christians that there will be justice for all deeds. However, this justice will be as God plans, not as man prefers.

Discussion Questions

1. What is your favorite imprecatory psalm by David?

2. Is it sinful to ask God, "How long?" Why or why not?

3. Mosaic Law required stoning for adulterers. Was this fair justice then? Fair justice now?

4. How did Jesus apply Matthew 5:38–42 in His life?

5. Describe meekness in our contemporary lifestyles.

6. In Romans 12:18, why is the commandment "live peaceably with all men" delimited by the phrase "as depends on you?"

7. Why will every tongue confess God on judgment day?

8. In Revelation 21:7, what does it mean to be God's son?

9. Why doesn't God ensure justice for us while we live on earth?

Evangelism

Rivers of water run down from my eyes, Because men do not keep Your law. My zeal has consumed me, because my enemies have forgotten Your words (Ps. 119:136, 139).

Lesson 15: Evangelism

In the 1st century, Jews were so immersed in the Mosaic Law's sacrificial system that many could not accept Christ's sacrifice. Neither could the Gentiles give up their idols and culture for the gospel. Significant change for Jew or Gentile was not easy because religious and business practices were tied together in ancient cultures.

For example, the temple of Diana in Ephesus served many purposes besides worship to the goddess Diana. The temple was beautiful and one of the seven wonders of the ancient world. The temple was a bank, a refuge for criminals, and the sponsor for superstitious charms. The Ephesian community of silversmiths made an excellent living crafting

Diana shrines for visitors of the city and temple and caused civil unrest to stop gospel teaching *(Acts 19:21–41).*

The Jewish culture had roadblocks for Christian evangelism. Jewish life centered around the temple and the related religious practices. Jewish leaders threatened the people with excommunication from all Jewish rituals for believing in Jesus Christ. Excommunication resulted in being cut off from all social, religious, and business communication with the whole nation. The richest to the poorest of the Jewish people dreaded this sentence. Excommunication as a tool to control the Jewish population is specifically mentioned four times in the book of John.

However, no one spoke openly of Him for fear of the Jews (John 7:13).

His parents answered them and said, "We know that this is our son, and that he was born blind; but by what means he now sees we do not know, or who opened his eyes we do not know. He is of age; ask him. He will speak for himself." His parents said these things because they feared the Jews, for the Jews had agreed already that if anyone confessed that He was Christ, he would be put out of the synagogue (John 9:20–22).

Nevertheless even among the rulers many believed in Him, but because of the Pharisees they did not confess Him, lest they should be put out of the synagogue; for they loved the praise of men more than the praise of God (John 12:42–43).

After this, Joseph of Arimathea, being a disciple of Jesus, but secretly, for fear of the Jews, asked Pilate that he might take away the body of Jesus; and Pilate gave him permission. So he came and took the body of Jesus. And Nicodemus, who at first came to Jesus by night, also came, bringing a mixture of myrrh and aloes, about a hundred pounds (John 19:38–39).

The psalmist had tears in his eyes because men were not obedient to God, and he had the zeal to explain God's laws to his enemies. Christians are to have the same care, passion, and enthusiasm to teach others about Christianity.

Jesus's Great Commission

And Jesus came and spoke to them, saying, "All authority has been given to Me in heaven and on earth. Go therefore and make disciples of all the nations, baptizing them in the name of the Father and of the Son and of the Holy Spirit, teaching them to observe all things that I have commanded you; and lo, I am with you always, even to the end of the age" (Matt. 28:18–20).

In Matthew 28, Jesus is speaking to the eleven loyal disciples and 500 more people *(1 Cor. 15:6).* who had followed them to Galilee. Jesus declares His authority, and then the conclusion of that authority are these commands.

Go therefore and make disciples of all the nations

Baptizing them in the name of the Father and of the Son and of the Holy Spirit,

Teaching them to observe all things that I have commanded you (Matt. 28:19-20a).

Christians cannot deny that Jesus meant for us to tell others about the gospel. The gospel is for people of all nations and requires baptism and obedience. God wants all people to believe and follow Him and always has. He created man in His image and said, "It is good." He walked in the garden with Adam and Eve until their disobedience resulted in the eviction. Even then, God provided for mankind to be with Him.

However, the gospel is the lightest burden leading to living in God's presence. We are just required to believe and obey. To believe and obey, we must hear the gospel. To hear requires that someone tell us. Jesus said, "Go and make disciples." Our eyes must cry because others do not know the gospel, so that we go and tell them. This desire and the resulting action is Jesus's great commission.

Obstacles

Most of us have many reasons why we do not mention our faith to others. At times, we do not even recognize the opportunity! We are confident that our modern times make it harder to teach others of Christ than during the first century. Let's consider the obstacle to teaching the gospel in Ephesus for comparison.

- Ephesus was commercially prominent. Three highways from Colossae and Laodicea (Eastern trade), Galatia thru Sardis (Asia Minor), and the south (Meander Valley). led into the city and a large harbor. Prosperity and self-reliance cause many to doubt their need for God.

- Ephesus was politically important. The city was a free-city without Roman soldiers garrisoned there. It had a democratically elected governing body with a regular assembly of citizens and was an assize town where the Roman governor regularly heard and tried important cases. Keeping the status quo with Rome was essential to maintaining these privileges.

- Ephesus was religiously significant and had multiple temples for many gods. All temple worship involved prostitution and frenzied worship services. The temple for Diana was most prominent and well known. The month of May was sacred to Diana, and the annual Pan-Ionian games occurred in that month. Idolatry and temple worship supported many financial obligations for the city.

- The Ephesian people had the reputation of being fickle, superstitious, and immoral. They were not the type of people to be interested in or interested by godly people.

Ephesus was an immoral city with so many reasons not to embrace Christianity, with many undesirable and wicked people living there. Still, Paul visited the city multiple times. He opened his letter to the Ephesians with *"to the saints who are in Ephesus and faithful in Christ Jesus"* (Eph. 1:1b).

Paul was just one man yet found Ephesians to teach the gospel. These Ephesians had so many worldly reasons to disregard Paul's teaching.

However, Paul taught them, and they listened and obeyed. He did not consider the obstacles to teaching the Ephesians as too hard to overcome. He knew each Ephesian was worthy of hearing the gospel and proceeded in that manner.

Today we are very removed from the Ephesian culture. These days, immorality is not clothed in temple worship, but it is the same as the Ephesian immorality. Business, political, religious, and family issues are part of everyone's life then and now. All Ephesian obstacles are relevant now, but present themselves differently in today's culture.

Paul understood the Ephesian obstacles to teach the gospel and still boldly taught the Ephesians. Today, we can also boldly teach. All people have hindrances to obeying the gospel. Be like Paul and teach them anyway!

Preparation

Jesus lived in an agrarian culture, and His listeners understood farming analogies. Today, we can understand this simple analogy to farming and

evangelism. Farming requires planning and preparation, but first, the farmer must intend to plant the field. All the seed, machinery, and planning is void without the intention and determination that a field needs planting. We are like the farmer; we must purposely determine that we will teach another person the gospel.

Jesus told His disciple to look at all people as someone to teach: "Behold, I say to you, lift up your eyes and look at the fields, for they are already white for harvest!" He warned them that now was the time and not four months later *(John 4:35)*. The first step to evangelism is determining that we can and will teach someone else.

The next step to teaching is knowing what we believe. We do not have to know every verse in the Bible, nor have an immediate answer to any argument someone may have. However, we must have confidence in our faith and spend time in our Bibles to grow our knowledge in our faith. We must be like the Bereans who searched the Scriptures daily *(Acts 17:11)*.

In context, the Bereans were hearing the gospel from Paul and Silas, not teaching. However, no one can teach without knowledge of their subject. We must study the Scriptures for ourselves as the Bereans did. This preparation gets us ready to tell someone else what we believe.

Preach the word! Be ready in season and out of season. Convince, rebuke, exhort, with all longsuffering and teaching (2 Tim. 4:2).

Our study of the Scriptures prepares us to teach whenever opportunities arise. With no intent or preparation to teach or plant, there will be no teaching or planting. We must intend to plant the field before we can ever place seeds in the dirt. We can teach no one if we do not prepare ourselves with the intention of teaching someone else.

Paul counsels Timothy to be ready to preach the gospel at every opportunity. Be like Timothy, prepared to preach the word!

Action, Action, Action

In Peter's letter to the Christians facing difficulties and discrimination in the first century, Peter declared that all Christians must be ready to tell others of their faith. His declaration was firm even though these Christians were facing lethal persecution for their Christian faith.

Always be ready to give a defense to everyone who asks you a reason for the hope that is in you, with meekness and fear (1 Pet. 3:15b).

Evangelism requires action even when it is hard to do, but Christians do not do all the work themselves. God only expects us to plant and water! He expects us to do what we can with what we have and helps us along the way.

I planted, Apollos watered, but God gave the increase. So then neither he who plants is anything, nor he who waters, but God who gives the increase (1 Cor. 3:6–7).

We must teach when we can with the skills and abilities that God has given us. We may not be a preacher, but God expects us to talk to others of our faith. Some commentaries suggest Paul suffered from stage fright and was fully or partially blind. However, Paul knew he had to preach the gospel and teach others of Christ. These verses support these conclusions of Paul's infirmities and his preparation to teach others despite those infirmities.

Then Paul dwelt two whole years in his own rented house, and received all who came to him, preaching the kingdom of God and teaching the things which concern the Lord Jesus Christ with all confidence (Acts 28:30–31).

"For his letters, " they say, "are weighty and powerful, but his bodily presence is weak, and his speech contemptible" (2 Cor. 10:10).

Even though I am untrained in speech, yet I am not in knowledge. But we have been thoroughly manifested among you in all things (2 Cor. 11:6).

You know that because of physical infirmity I preached the gospel to you at the first. And my trial which was in my flesh you did not despise or reject, but you received me as an angel of God, even as Christ Jesus. What then was the blessing you enjoyed? For I bear you witness that, if possible, you would have plucked out your own eyes and given them to me (Gal. 4:13–15).

Paul overcame any stage fright and blindness with preparation for his sermons and lessons. He made himself a formidable teacher of the gospel. He did not hand-pick the people that he would teach or preach only in selected places. Paul taught whoever was with him wherever they were.

He preached in synagogues wherever he traveled, in the Jerusalem temple, at the river bank by Philippi *(Acts 16:11–15),* in front of many governing bodies, at the Areopagus in Athens *(Acts 17:22–32),* while making tents *(Acts 18:3–4),* in the middle of the night *(Acts 20:7–9),* on stairs of army barracks *(Acts 21:40),* while awaiting trial in Rome *(Acts 28:30–31),* and wherever else he found himself. He taught Sergius Paulus, against the wishes of a false prophet *(Acts 13:6–12),* the priest of Zeus and other citizens of Lystra *(Acts 13:8–18),* jailers *(Acts 16:25–34),* Governor Felix *(Acts 24:24),* Governor Festus and King Agrippa *(Acts 26:1–32),* the household of Caesar *(Phil. 4:22),* and whoever he found himself talking.

Paul used his own advice given in 2 Timothy 4:2. He had told Timothy to be ready at all times to teach and preach. Paul put his own words into action. He taught whoever was around him, wherever he was. He preached early in the day and late at night and did not let his shortcomings stop him from doing God's work. Paul assumed anytime was a good time to tell the world about the gospel.

Warning

2 Peter chapter 2 is devoted to warning us about false teaching. He writes of their destructive and deceptive doctrines and their doom. We must be like the Bereans and study the Scriptures ourselves to know

gospel teaching is true and ensure that we teach the truth. We must only teach Christ's gospel, as any other gospel is false.

> *According to the grace of God which was given to me, as a wise master builder I have laid the foundation, and another builds on it. But let each one take heed how he builds on it. For no other foundation can anyone lay than that which is laid, which is Jesus Christ* (1 Cor. 3:10–11).

Summary

God commanded all Christians to teach others about the gospel. We must study ourselves to prepare to teach another. All individuals have obstacles to hearing and obeying the gospel. A preacher and teacher of the gospel preaches and teaches anyway.

Discussion Questions

1. What reasons would John have to mention Jewish excommunication so many times?

2. How can each of us implement Jesus's great commission?

3. What considerations might Paul have had to teach the Ephesians about the gospel?

4. What are our obstacles to teaching today?

5. How can we prepare to evangelize?

6. How does knowledge of our faith help us to evangelize?

7. How did Paul's letters to Timothy prepare Timothy to preach?

8. How is 1 Peter 3:15 relevant to teaching the gospel?

9. How is Apollos an example of good evangelism when he was incorrectly teaching baptism in Acts 18:24–28?

10. How is Paul an excellent example of evangelism?

11. Why are we warned only to preach the true gospel?

God Is Love

My soul clings to the dust; Revive me according to Your word… Behold, I long for Your precepts; Revive me in Your righteousness… Consider how I love Your precepts; Revive me, O Lord, according to Your lovingkindness (Ps. 119:25, 40, 159).

Lesson 16: God Is Love

Pop culture shouts, "God is love!" meaning God is love without any fearsomeness. This God only wants His people to be happy, just as an indulgent parent spoils his or her children. He is benevolent with shiny lovingkindness oozing everywhere without any demands of His people.

Our real God is love—true love. His lovingkindness has extended to mankind since time began. He made Adam and Eve clothes from animal skins when they discovered they were naked and covered themselves

with leaves. He sent angels to evacuate Lot and his family from Sodom before the city's destruction. He forgave Peter for denying Him three times in the high priest's courtyard. God made man in His image and loves His creation.

God's love is not conditional, as He always loves us. However, God has expectations for us and expects His people to love and obey Him. He had told Adam and Eve not to eat fruit from or touch the Tree of Knowledge of Good and Evil. He expelled them from Eden for their disobedience. The angels warned Lot and his family not to look back at the destruction of Sodom. Lot's wife turned into a pillar of salt for her disobedience. Peter lived long enough to repent for his sin and continued his work spreading the gospel for many years. God is love, but He has expectations for His people.

Therefore know that the Lord your God, He is God, the faithful God who keeps covenant and mercy for a thousand generations with those who love Him and keep His commandments (Deut. 7:9)

The Bible Tells Us So

There is a children's song that says, "Jesus loves me, this I know, for the Bible tells me so." The innocence of children knows the lyrics are truthful and sweetly sing about the love of God. Children are confident of God's love and care for them. Yes, the Bible tells us that God is love, and love comes from God.

Beloved, let us love one another, for love is of God; and everyone who loves is born of God and knows God. He who does not love does not know God, for God is love (1 John 4:7–8).

God's love is so much more than a pop culture slogan. Pop culture limits God to only this one characteristic. The Bible tells us of many attributes of God. Looking only in the first half of Psalm 119, we see these qualities of God.

He has righteous judgments *(v. 7)*, He deals bountifully with His people *(v. 17)*, He has wondrous things in His law *(v. 18)*, He rebukes those who stray from His commands *(v. 21)*, He helps us understand His precepts *(v. 27)*, He is gracious *(v. 29)*, His is the way of truth *(v. 30)*, There is salvation in His word *(v. 41)*, He is our comfort *(v. 50)*, He is merciful *(v. 64)*, He is good and does good *(v. 68)*, He created us *(v. 73)*, He is faithful *(v. 75)*, and He is kind *(v. 76)*.

God, who loves us and is love, is omnipotent and omnipresent, and omniscient. He commands us, rebukes us, and is righteous, gracious, truthful, merciful, good, kind, and faithful. This powerful God is the God of which the children sing because the Bible tells us so.

God's Expectations

What does the powerful God in the children's song want from the people on earth? God has always been clear in His expectations and commandments. He ordered Adam and Eve to avoid the tree of knowledge of good and evil. Eve understood this command and told the serpent so. God instructed the ancient patriarchs in what they should do and later gave the Law to Moses. In Deuteronomy, God's Law tells us this.

And now, Israel, what does the Lord your God require of you, but to fear the Lord your God, to walk in all His ways and to love Him, to serve the Lord your God with all your heart and with all your soul, and to keep

the commandments of the Lord and His statutes which I command you today for your good? (Deut. 10:12–13).

God loves His people but has requirements for them, too. The above verses summarize all of God's expectations of His people. Respect, love, obedience, and dedication are the only things God expects from us!

God added one more expectation when Jesus came to earth. He requires faith that Jesus is Christ and the Son of God. God's love for us graciously sent Jesus to be the final sacrifice for our sins.

Whoever confesses that Jesus is the Son of God, God abides in him, and he in God. And we have known and believed the love that God has for us. God is love, and he who abides in love abides in God, and God in him. Love has been perfected among us in this: that we may have boldness in the day of judgment; because as He is, so are we in this world (1 John 4:15–17).

God has requirements and expectations for His people, and the Bible tells me so.

God's Lovingkindness

The author of Psalm 119 prayed for God to revive him during his trials and needed God's lovingkindness every day. Lovingkindness is tenderness and consideration toward others. The psalmist wanted God to pick him up from the dust of his life with gentleness. We do not know the specifics of the writer's problems or the poetic license taken in the psalm. We know that the writer realized that he needed God and His lovingkindness to the bones of his soul.

David's confidence in God's faithfulness and lovingkindness is the basis of many psalms. He praises God at all times and asks for God's continued blessings. A few examples follow.

• Psalm 3 praises God and asks for help as David is fleeing from his son, Absalom.

I cried to the Lord with my voice, And He heard me from His holy hill. Selah… I lay down and slept; I awoke, for the Lord sustained me… Salvation belongs to the Lord. Your blessing is upon Your people. Selah (vv. 4, 5, 8).

- Psalm 4 asserts that only God provides joy and safety.

You have put gladness in my heart, More than in the season that their grain and wine increased. I will both lie down in peace, and sleep; For You alone, O Lord, make me dwell in safety (vv. 7–8).

- Psalm 18 assures us that God delivered David from Saul.

The Lord lives! Blessed be my Rock! Let the God of my salvation be exalted. It is God who avenges me, And subdues the peoples under me; He delivers me from my enemies. You also lift me up above those who rise against me; You have delivered me from the violent man (vv. 46–48).

- Psalm 34 praises God when David had to pretend to be crazy before Abimelech.

I will bless the Lord at all times; His praise shall continually be in my mouth… I sought the Lord, and He heard me, And delivered me from all my fears… The eyes of the Lord are on the righteous, And His ears are open to their cry… The Lord redeems the soul of His servants, And none of those who trust in Him shall be condemned (vv. 1, 4, 15, 22).

David was a king and a warrior. However, he needed God's lovingkindness every day. David wanted the gentle touch of his powerful God, not the wrath of His punishment. David knew that God is merciful and loving to those that love Him. This mercy and love are available to us today.

But God, who is rich in mercy, because of His great love with which He loved us, even when we were dead in trespasses, made us alive together with Christ (by grace you have been saved) (Eph. 2:4–5).

But as it is written: "Eye has not seen, nor ear heard, Nor have entered into the heart of man The things which God has prepared for those who love Him" (1 Cor. 2:9).

David is an excellent example of confidence in God. He depended on God's lovingkindness while he fled from enemies and when he was safe. David knew that God loved him and would be with him in all circumstances. David knew this during his lifetime, and the Bible tells us so in our lifetimes.

God's Love Commands

Our God is love and commands His people to love—to love Him and to love others. Love is the greatest commandment given to us by God.

"And you shall love the Lord your God with all your heart, with all your soul, with all your mind, and with all your strength." This is the first commandment. And the second, like it, is this: "You shall love your neighbor as yourself." There is no other commandment greater than these (Mark 12:30–31).

The essence of these two New Testament commands is to love God and love each other. Love is the fundamental idea! God loved us enough to provide and sacrifice for us. He knew that man's sins would eternally separate man from Him. God, who is everything, sacrificed a part of Himself as payment for our sins. His example shows us how to love others selflessly.

In this the love of God was manifested toward us, that God has sent His only begotten Son into the world, that we might live through Him. In this is love, not that we loved God, but that He loved us and sent His Son to be the propitiation for our sins. Beloved, if God so loved us, we also ought to love one another (1 John 4:9–11).

This biblical love for others is *agapē* love, not romantic love, close friendship, or brotherly love. It is goodwill and benevolence for other people. 1 Corinthians 13 describes *agapē* love very well. Love will endure when faith and hope are no longer needed.

Love suffers long and is kind; love does not envy; love does not parade itself, is not puffed up; does not behave rudely, does not seek its own, is not provoked, thinks no evil; does not rejoice in iniquity, but rejoices in the truth; bears all things, believes all things, hopes all things, endures all things. Love never fails (1 Cor. 13:4–8a).

Love will never fail. The Bible tells us so!

The Burden of God's Commandments

It is hard to give 100% all the time. At times, the apostles murmured, questioned, and made mistakes. They lived with Jesus but fell below the mark in their faith and actions. For example, Peter suggested tabernacles be built to worship Moses and Elijah at Jesus's transfiguration. Peter,

James, and John fell asleep in the Garden of Gethsemane when asked to wait for Jesus to pray.

These heroes of faith stumbled on occasion. Yet, the Bible tells us that the burden of obeying the gospel is light and not burdensome.

Come to Me, all you who labor and are heavy laden, and I will give you rest. Take My yoke upon you and learn from Me, for I am gentle and lowly in heart, and you will find rest for your souls. For My yoke is easy and My burden is light (Matt. 11:28–30).

For this is the love of God, that we keep His commandments. And His commandments are not burdensome (1 John 5:3).

The Jews had been given a heavy burden under the Mosiac Law, demanding perfection from the law keepers. Jesus assures them that God's grace and mercy provide rest from this weight. With Jesus sharing our yokes, we find our burdens of disease, sorrow, financial distress, and insecurity easier to bear.

Christ's commandments are not burdensome, as was the Old Law, but free us to be better people, holy people. God's love sustains Christians walking the narrow path. We show our love for God by keeping His commandments. His grace abounds to forgive our sins and shortcomings as we travel to the strait gate *(Rom. 5:20–6:2).* The Bible tells us so.

Man's Assurance of God's Love

Many marriage vows promise to love till death parts the husband and wife but end in acrimony and divorce. How do we know God's promise to love us is better?

God has kept all His promises—every one of them! His first promise was to Satan, who tricked Adam and Eve to eat the fruit *(Gen. 3:15).* God promised Satan that woman's seed would bruise his head. The birth, death, and resurrection of Jesus Christ fulfilled this promise and defeated Satan. God's land, seed, and nation promise to Abraham first occurred while Abraham was a nomad without children. God kept all these promises as well. God has kept every promise made in the Old Testament.

We are promised God's love many times in the New Testament. The evidence of this love is Christ's sacrifice for each of us.

He who did not spare His own Son, but delivered Him up for us all, how shall He not with Him also freely give us all things? (Rom. 8:32).

For I am persuaded that neither death nor life, nor angels nor principalities nor powers, nor things present nor things to come, nor height nor depth, nor any other created thing, shall be able to separate us from the love of God which is in Christ Jesus our Lord (Rom. 8:38–39).

I have been crucified with Christ; it is no longer I who live, but Christ lives in me; and the life which I now live in the flesh I live by faith in the Son of God, who loved me and gave Himself for me (Gal. 2:20).

God has assured us that He loves us and gave Christ as the final proof of this love. Nothing can separate us from God's love, and the Bible tells us so.

Summary

God's love is everlasting for all people. He requires that we respect Him, obey Him, serve Him, and love Him to show our love for Him. God's gentleness and lovingkindness support us through life's trials and are promised to us forever.

Discussion Questions

1. How does God's treatment of Adam and Eve, Lot and his family, and Peter show His faithfulness and love?

2. What Bible verse describes God best to you?

3. Does God's commands in Deuteronomy 10:12–13 apply to us today? Why or why not?

4. How do we experience God's lovingkindness today?

5. In what ways are God's greatest commandments hard to obey?

   In what ways are they easy to obey?

6. How is Jesus's death an example of God's lovingkindness?

7. Why will love endure when faith and hope are no longer needed?

8. How does Jesus's yoke lighten our burden?

9. When is keeping God's commandments burdensome for you?

    What should you do to bring your life in line with 1 John 5:3?

10.   What are your favorite verses about God's love?

Mercy and Forgiveness

Deal with Your servant according to Your mercy, and teach me Your statutes. I am Your servant; Give me understanding, that I may know Your testimonies (Ps. 119:124–125).

Lesson 17: Mercy and Forgiveness

Forgiveness and mercy are essential to Christians. We need forgiveness and mercy from God for our sins against Him. We desire forgiveness and mercy from other people for our wrongdoings against them. Plus, we must forgive and be merciful to other people for offenses made to us.

Forgiveness and mercy are critical to us when desired for our crimes and often less important when requested by others for their misdeeds.

- Mercy is compassion and love expressed with action or undeserved favor, especially when mercy is to someone that a person has power over.

- Forgiveness is not holding trespasses against a person or pardoning someone of wrongdoing.

Some people consider forgiveness and mercy from others as their right to smooth over any transgression they have made. Others see forgiveness and mercy as unattainable prizes for even the smallest fault. Most people struggle with giving and accepting forgiveness and mercy in their life and understanding forgiveness and mercy from God.

We have seen persons on the news telling of their forgiveness of the criminal who caused them harm. Did you wonder how they could do that? All of us strain to forgive others and to offer mercy. Those people are straining, too. However, at that moment, I believe their forgiveness is real, while their pain remains vast.

How often have you reflected on memories of past misdeeds against you? These misdeeds can be slight or grievous. Still, the memories come back into our minds for reconsideration, whether beckoned or not. Lately, memories like these have crept into my thoughts for situations that I would have professed I had forgiven. Had my forgiveness been real, or was I sinning by not forgiving? After all, the Bible says,

> For if you forgive men their trespasses, your heavenly Father will also forgive you. But if you do not forgive men their trespasses, neither will your Father forgive your trespasses (Matt. 6:14–15).

We all want God's mercy and forgiveness. In Matthew 6, we see that God wants His people also to have mercy and forgiveness for others.

Our Mercy and Forgiveness

The people on the news and I have at least one thing in common. We remember the trespasses against us. We forgave someone for the sin against us yesterday, but our memories of that sin haunt us today. Those same memories may float into our thoughts tomorrow and again the following week. Consider the verses in Matthew 18.

> Then Peter came to Him and said, "Lord, how often shall my brother sin against me, and I forgive him? Up to seven times?" Jesus said to him, "I do not say to you, up to seven times, but up to seventy times seven" (Matt. 18:21–22).

In New Testament times, the number seven had a lot of symbolism. Seven was considered the perfect divine number, indicated wholeness, and was the most sacred number among the Hebrews. Ten was a number of completeness. Since seventy is seven times ten, seventy would be divinely complete. By understanding the symbolism of Hebrew numbers, it is clear Jesus is not telling Peter that we must forgive someone 490 times. We must continually forgive them!

If forgiveness is an ongoing requirement for people, no wonder we struggle with forgiveness! Those people on the news and I will have to forgive others for their sins against us repeatedly. Not only will we forgive once, but we must forgive every time we remember the trespass. Seventy times seven is a lot of forgiving!

Let's go back to the previous example of the persons on the news who were expressing forgiveness for a criminal who had injured them. As time goes on, they are going to feel grief over the loss or injury caused by that criminal. The prior forgiveness did not remove their memories, repair the damage, or repay the loss. Those grieving people must live with the results of the criminal's actions, and they must also continually forgive the criminal. That is how seventy times seven works!

Most of us think of mercy as in a movie script. For instance, a criminal faces a deserved sentence from the judge and begs for mercy to obtain a lesser punishment for his crime. The criminal deserves a life sentence, but hopes for a shorter time in prison.

Mercy could be that the judge sentences the criminal to 10 years in prison instead of the deserved life sentence.

Mercy is not only a movie script but a part of our lives. Our mercy to others is not required only in large trespasses against us but the small ones too. The compassion and love of mercy are evident in people's actions every day. For example,

- We can offer help to someone in need. The assistance may be a meal, lawn care, babysitting, or a loan of money or property.

- We can resist the opportunities to rehash the misdeeds of others. Past transgressions of our spouses, children, family, and friends require our mercy. Even mercy during discussions of these misdeeds is essential.

- We can refrain from taunting someone after we are proven right.

Our mercy to others is love in action, and God commands it.

Woe to you, scribes and Pharisees, hypocrites! For you pay tithe of mint and anise and cummin, and have neglected the weightier matters of the law: justice and mercy and faith. These you ought to have done, without leaving the others undone (Matt. 23:23).

Verse 23 is the fourth condemnation that Jesus states for the scribes and Pharisees in this chapter of Matthew. The scribes and Pharisees see themselves as hyper-religious and hold themselves above the other Jewish people in the keeping of the Law and other traditions. It was more important to count the flakes of spice to ensure an accurate tithe than to perform acts of mercy in their community. Jesus emphasizes that mercy is more important than a tithe of mint. How we treat others is vital!

We find an example of forgiveness and mercy in the letters to the Corinthians. A man had taken his father's wife which was a sin not even tolerated among the pagan Gentiles *(1 Cor. 5:1).* Paul commanded the

Corinthians to discipline this man to save his soul *(1 Cor. 5:5)*. In 2 Corinthians, Paul urges forgiveness and mercy to this same man, because the man had repented of his sin.

> *This punishment which was inflicted by the majority is sufficient for such a man, so that, on the contrary, you ought rather to forgive and comfort him, lest perhaps such a one be swallowed up with too much sorrow. Therefore I urge you to reaffirm your love to him (2 Cor. 2:6–8).*

Forgiveness and mercy from the Corinthian brethren to the repentant man was necessary and desired by God. Forgiveness is one of the most repeated themes in the Bible. A forgiving attitude by each person to others is essential to be pleasing to God.

> *Bearing with one another, and forgiving one another, if anyone has a complaint against another; even as Christ forgave you, so you also must do (Col. 3:13).*

God's Mercy and Forgiveness

God commands us to forgive others. Remember, in Matthew 6:14–15; we must forgive others to be forgiven by God? Remember how we can forgive and cannot forget, and so, must forgive over and over *(Matt.*

18:21–22)? God's forgiveness is once and done. Once God has forgiven sin, He forgets it!

> *This is the covenant that I will make with them after those days, says the Lord: "I will put My laws into their hearts, and in their minds I will write them, " then He adds, "Their sins and their lawless deeds I will remember no more" (Heb. 10:16–17).*

Mercy is undeserved favor to someone when the mercy-giver has power over that person. God certainly has all authority and control over humanity! One of His greatest mercies to us is His forgiveness of our sins against Him. When God forgives a person, He forgets that particular sin. He does not rehash that sin later, nor does He consider that sin when we commit new sins. He is not like us with our sleepless nights while we wrestle with past misdeeds against us. God's forgiveness is absolute and complete.

Men always want fairness and justice for misdeeds against them. Equity in all injustices is the utopia sought by many. God wants fairness and justice also. However, God's mercy is available to all people who ask for forgiveness of their sins against Him. His mercy is accessible to everyone who asks for forgiveness.

For I will be merciful to their unrighteousness, and their sin and their lawless deeds I will remember no more (Heb. 8:12).

God could seek justice for all our sins and condemn each sinner. God's condemnation would have no appeal and no higher court to review the sentence. God's mercy gives up this opportunity for justice against the sinner and, instead, forgives them of the sin.

Our salvation is rooted in God's forgiveness: "for all have sinned and fall short of the glory of God" *(Rom. 3:23).* All people have sinned and will continue to sin. God's greatest mercy to repentant man is His forgiveness of our sin.

Must We Ask for Forgiveness and Mercy to Obtain Them?

Often, people believe that individuals are not required to forgive another unless the sinning person has asked for forgiveness.

- Let us start with Luke 17:3–4 to demonstrate that a person must request forgiveness before forgiveness is required.

Take heed to yourselves. If your brother sins against you, rebuke him; and if he repents, forgive him. And if he sins against you seven times in a day, and seven times in a day returns to you, saying, "I repent, " you shall forgive him (Luke 17:3–4).

In these verses, the sinning brother asks for forgiveness.

- Similarly to this sinning brother of Luke 17, people must confess their sins and repent before God forgives their sins.

If we confess our sins, He is faithful and just to forgive us our sins and to cleanse us from all unrighteousness (1 John 1:9).

- A third verse in this argument tells us to forgive others as God has forgiven us. So, if God forgives those who ask, then we must forgive those who ask us.

Therefore, as the elect of God, holy and beloved, put on tender mercies, kindness, humility, meekness, longsuffering; bearing with one another, and forgiving one another, if anyone has a complaint against another; even as Christ forgave you, so you also must do (Col. 3:12–13).

Often, the conclusion from these verses is that a sinning person must ask for forgiveness before the sinned-against person is required to forgive.

God wants us to forgive when asked; however, He requires a forgiving spirit from all His people. He wants a forgiving spirit to be a mark of His people. My daughter-in-law once said that you have to forgive and let it go, or the sin against you will eat you up. The people in the lesson's first example knew this when they forgave the criminal. The New Testament teaches a merciful, loving spirit for God's people throughout its chapters. For example:

And whenever you stand praying, if you have anything against anyone, forgive him, that your Father in heaven may also forgive you your trespasses. But if you do not forgive, neither will your Father in heaven forgive your trespasses (Mark 11:25–26).

Let all bitterness, wrath, anger, clamor, and evil speaking be put away from you, with all malice. And be kind to one another, tenderhearted, forgiving one another, even as God in Christ forgave you (Eph. 4:31–32).

But I say to you, love your enemies and pray for those who persecute you (Matt. 5:44).

A new commandment I give to you, that you love one another; as I have loved you, that you also love one another (John 13:34).

Blessed are the merciful, for they shall receive mercy (Matt. 5:7).

The story of the stoning of Stephen contains a wonderful example of a forgiving spirit. As Stephen is dying, he said, "Lord, do not charge them with this sin" (Acts 7:60b). Stephen forgave the people who were killing him!

In Luke 23, Jesus is hanging on the cross between two thieves. Before His crucifixion, a disciple betrayed Him, another disciple denied Him three times, and He had three illegal trials and several beatings. Jesus's forgiving spirit is evident in His words from the cross. He said, "Father, forgive them, for they do not know what they do" (Luke 23:34). Jesus wanted forgiveness for all those who had sinned against Him! None of the individuals involved in any of the activities against Jesus asked Him for forgiveness at the time that He was forgiving. What would Jesus do? He would forgive.

Summary

God desires His people to be merciful and to have a forgiving spirit. He demands that we forgive others for their wrongdoings against us to have forgiveness for our sins against Him.

Discussion Questions

1. Why is it desirable to forgive others?

    Must this forgiveness be expressed to the one receiving forgiveness?

2. Is it desirable to obtain forgiveness from someone? Why or why not?

3. Why does Jesus teach that we must continually forgive others?

4. Which is harder, mercy to others or mercy to yourself, and why?

5. Are God's forgiveness and mercy more than a human's? Why or why not.

6. Why is it important to understand that God has power over mankind when He is offering mercy and forgiveness?

7. Why does the author consider God's forgiveness to be mercy?

8. Does God require someone to ask for your forgiveness before God requires your forgiveness?

9. What does Luke 17:3–4 teach you about forgiveness?

CPSIA information can be obtained
at www.ICGtesting.com
Printed in the USA
BVHW021229080722
641542BV00006B/23

9 781584 275411